Making Memories

WITH FABRIC, PHOTOS, AND FAMILY KEEPSAKES

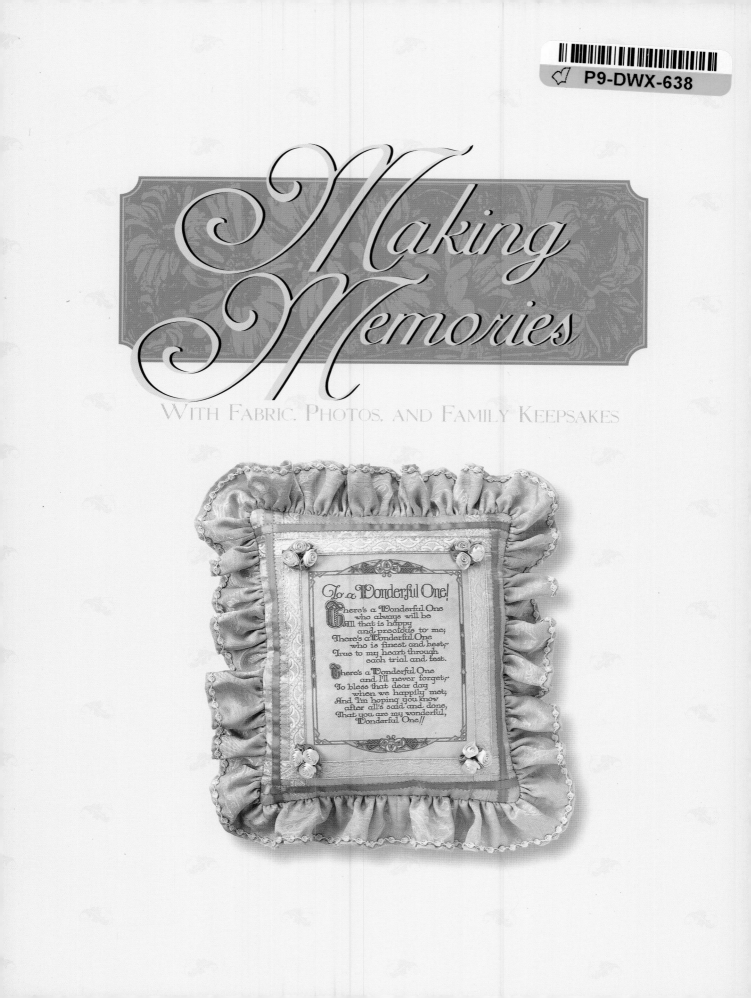

MARGARET SINDELAR

Making Memories
WITH FABRIC, PHOTOS, AND FAMILY KEEPSAKES

Copyright © 1998 by Landauer Corporation

This book was designed and produced by Landauer Books
A division of Landauer Corporation
12251 Maffitt Road, Cumming, Iowa 50061

President: Jeramy Lanigan Landauer
Vice President: Becky Johnston
Managing Editor: Marlene Hemberger Heuertz
Editor: Mary V. Green
Art Director: Robert Mickey Hager
Cover Design: Tracy DeVenney
Associate Editor: Sarah Reid
Technical Illustrator: Stan Green/Green Graphics
Graphics Technician: Stewart Cott
Creative Assistant: Laurel Albright
Photographers: Craig Anderson, Amy Cooper, and Dennis Kennedy

Martingale
& COMPANY

Published by Martingale & Company
PO Box 118, Bothell, WA 98041-0118 USA

Pastimes™

This book is printed on acid-free paper.
Printed in Hong Kong

Library of Congress Cataloging-in-Publication Data Available on Request.

10 9 8 7 6 5 4 3 2 1

MARGARET SINDELAR

Making Memories

WITH FABRIC, PHOTOS, AND FAMILY KEEPSAKES

Martingale
& COMPANY

Contents

ANNIVERSARY
Forever Yours

WEDDING
From This Day Forward

BABY
A New Hand In Ours

FAMILY
Families Are Forever

GRADUATION
Reach for the Stars

REFERENCE
For Further Information

INTRODUCTION

Cherished memories can be yours forever in fabric! To celebrate those everyday moments so special to you, each chapter opens with a themed memory quilt and delightful companion projects to display your favorite family keepsakes.

The new fabric photo transfer methods make it easy to bring the pages of your scrapbook alive when you feature family photos, antique postcards, poems, birth and wedding certificates on many of the special occasion quilts. Traditional quilt patterns such as Double Wedding Ring, Tumbling Blocks, and Cathedral Windows are the basis for quilts and other creative expressions commemorating favorite holidays, vacations, anniversaries, a new baby, a graduate, and the bride and groom.

I hope that the wide variety of quilts and quick and easy projects on the following pages will be your inspiration for making memories...with fabric, photos, and family keepsakes!

Margaret Sindelar

back moments that mean the most

ANNIVERSARY

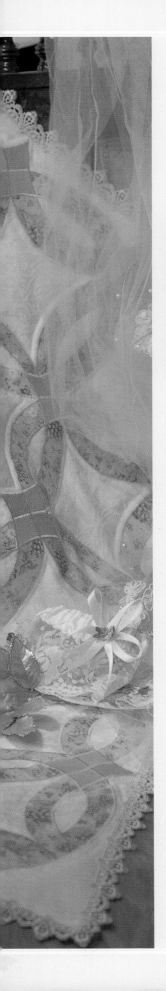

Forever Yours

An anniversary is a special reminder of the dreams we have gathered and the promises we have kept—to ourselves first and then to others. To commemorate this spirit of commitment and devotion, I've created an inspiring anniversary collection celebrating cherished quilted memories. On the following pages you'll find easy-to-adapt ideas for almost any wedding anniversary—from the first to the fiftieth!

The Double Wedding Ring quilt presents a perfect opportunity to frame a formal wedding portrait from the past in fabric to become a quilted memory for all time. Precious family memories can easily be displayed as fabric art using new techniques such as photo transfer paper. Even the traditional Double Wedding Ring works up quickly with simple appliqué and fusible web techniques.

To further preserve family history, the framed wedding invitation, below, is transformed into a work of art when surrounded by favorite family keepsakes.

The possibilities for creating quilted
memories from fabric with favorite
family photographs are almost endless.
Let your imagination be your guide!

or a special event, such as the 50th wedding anniversary, golden accents are a must for marking the milestone. Elegant moiré fabric adds the golden touch to the album cover, opposite.

Appropriately enough, Cathedral Windows is perfect for the featured block on this exquisite quilted keepsake.

This traditional pattern lends itself well to adaptations as shown on the sample block below. A quick-change of fabric color from gold to ruby red, and Cathedral Windows becomes four diamonds—just right for celebrating a 40th wedding anniversary!

The wedding ceremony followed by the first year of marriage often holds the fondest memories for newlyweds. Discover how easy it is to preserve "A Year of Happiness" with a machine-quilted fabric block with embroidery that serves as the background for a dozen miniature brass frames. Choose a miniature photo, charm, theater ticket stub, or other reminder of a special event for each month of that all important first year.

For an enduring first anniversary keepsake, transfer a few verses or a sentimental poem to fabric for a pillow poem that will be forever yours!

DOUBLE WEDDING RING ANNIVERSARY QUILT

27" x 33"

MATERIALS

- 1 yard of peach print fabric for patchwork

- 1 yard of cream damask fabric for background

- 1 yard of cream fabric for back

- ¼ yard of cream fabric for binding (optional)

- ⅛ yard each of peach solid and green solid fabrics for patchwork

- 10" x 12" piece of muslin for photo transfer

- 30" x 36" batting

- 5 yards of 1"-wide cream lace

- ½ yard of 7mm peach silk ribbon

- Peach rayon thread for machine appliqué

- Machine quilting thread

- Fusible web

- Photo transfer paper for color laser copiers*

- Fabric glue

- 8½" x 11" cardboard (optional)

*This project was made using Creative Copy Photo Transfer Paper by Quiltmakers. See Sources for details.

PREPARE THE APPLIQUÉS

1. Trace the quarter-ring pattern from below. Fold an 8½" x 11" sheet of paper into quarters as shown in Diagram A, and trace the pattern onto the paper. Keeping the paper folded, cut out the ring template. Unfold the template, and use it to trace 14 rings onto the paper side of the fusible web. If you want to make a sturdier template, glue the ring to a piece of cardboard and cut it out.

2. Cut out the rings, cutting slightly beyond the traced lines. Fuse the rings to the wrong side of the peach print fabric and cut along the traced lines.

3. Use the quarter-ring pattern to trace 28 quarter rings onto the paper side of the fusible web. Cut out beyond the lines. Fuse the quarter rings to the peach print fabric; cut out.

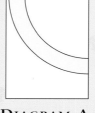

DIAGRAM A

4. Using the pattern on page 19, trace, fuse, and cut out 48 peach corner pieces and 48 green corner pieces.

APPLIQUÉ THE QUILT TOP

1. Cut a 30" x 36" rectangle from the cream damask fabric. Referring to Diagram B, arrange the rings on the damask, leaving an open area in the center that is approximately 9" x 14½". Check the placement carefully, making sure the overlap is equal on all rings. Fuse the rings in position.

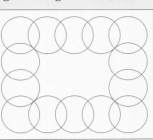

DIAGRAM B

2. Fuse the quarter-ring pieces to the quilt top to complete the interlocking ring pattern. See Diagram C.

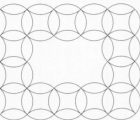

DIAGRAM C

3. Referring to Diagram D, fuse the peach and green corner pieces to the ring intersections.

4. Machine satin stitch around all the appliqués using peach rayon thread.

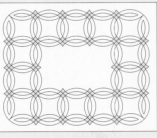

DIAGRAM D

FINISH THE QUILT

1. Layer the quilt top with batting and backing; baste. Machine quilt around the inside and outside of the rings.

2. Referring to the manufacturer's instructions, copy the photo onto the transfer paper. Cut out the photo, and follow instructions to iron it onto a slightly oversized piece of muslin.

3. Cut the photo transfer into an oval shape and use fabric glue to attach it to the center of the quilt. Stitch lace around the outside edge of the transfer to secure it.

4. Serge or clean-finish the outer edges of the quilt ½" beyond the wedding ring design. If you prefer a traditional binding, cut four 1½" x 44" strips from the cream fabric. Sew the short ends together to make one long strip. Fold the strip in half lengthwise, wrong sides together. Sew to the quilt top with a ¼" seam allowance, mitering the corners. Turn the folded edge to the back and whipstitch in place.

5. Topstitch the lace around the outside edge of the quilt. If you want to give the lace an antique look, tea-dye it by soaking it in hot tea for 20 minutes; rinse and allow to dry.

6. Thread the silk ribbon through the quilt below the photo, and tie wedding rings with a bow.

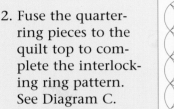

QUARTER RING PATTERN

CORNER PIECE

FRAMED INVITATION

MATERIALS

- Wedding invitation
- Assorted mementos
- Purchased frame with double mat
- Hand-marbled paper
- Spray adhesive
- Craft knife
- Cutting mat

ASSEMBLE THE FRAME

1. Spray the front of the inner mat with spray adhesive, following the manufacturer's instructions. Place the mat face down on the wrong side of an oversized piece of hand-marbled or other art paper.

2. Using a craft knife and working on a cutting mat or other protected surface, carefully trim the extra paper from around the outside of the mat. Cut around the inside to remove the paper from the opening.

3. Center the invitation in the inner mat. Arrange mementos around the invitation as desired. If you intend to replace the glass in the frame, you may not need to glue the items, as the pressure of the glass may be enough to hold them in place. Check to make sure items will fit into the reassembled frame. If you decide not to use the glass, choose items carefully, as they will have to be glued into place.

4. When all items are secured, reassemble the frame.

Celebrate almost any wedding anniversary by combining the time-honored Cathedral Windows with appropriate fabric color choices.

CATHEDRAL WINDOWS ALBUM COVER

MATERIALS

- ¾ yard of gold moiré fabric for cover and lining*
- ¼ yard of cream-and-gold print fabric for block
- ⅛ yard of olive fabric for block
- 10" x 19" piece of thin batting
- 1 yard of 1¼"-wide gold lace
- 1¾ yards of ⅛" piping cord
- Small ribbon roses to match
- 4 small gold charms or buttons
- 1¼" gold locket charm
- 8" x 9½" x 2" photo album

Adjust fabric color selections as desired. To celebrate a 25th anniversary, use silver; for a 40th anniversary use ruby red.

CUTTING

1. From the gold moiré fabric, cut two 10½" x 19½" rectangles, one for the cover and one for the lining. Cut two 6¾" x 10½" rectangles for the flaps. Cut 1½"-wide bias strips and sew together to make one strip approximately 63" long.

2. From the cream-and-gold print fabric, cut four 8½" squares.

3. From the olive fabric, cut four 2¾" squares.

MAKE THE CATHEDRAL WINDOWS BLOCK

1. Fold an 8½" square in half, right sides together, and stitch the short ends using a ¼" seam allowance. Without turning the square right side out, refold the fabric, bringing the raw edges together and matching the seams in the center. See Diagram E. Pin and stitch the seam, leaving an opening for turning.

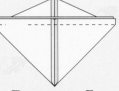

DIAGRAM E

2. Turn the square right side out through the opening; press. Referring to Diagram F, fold the four corners to the center so that the points meet in the middle; press. Repeat with the three remaining squares.

DIAGRAM F

3. Place two squares together with smooth sides facing. Unfold the same corner flap on each square and match the fold lines. Pin, then stitch together along the fold line. See Diagram G. Join the second pair of squares in the same manner. Pin the strips together and sew the adjoining flaps, creating a block.

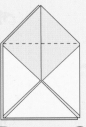

DIAGRAM G

4. Fold the corner flaps of each square back to its center; hand-stitch the four points together.

5. Center and pin a 2¾" olive square over each joining seam as shown in Diagram H. Fold the bias edges of the print fabric over the raw edges of the olive square and blind-stitch in place.

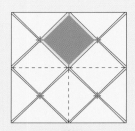

DIAGRAM H

ASSEMBLE THE ALBUM COVER

1. Position the block on the right side of one 10½" x 19½" moiré rectangle, with the right edge of the block ¼" from the right-hand edge of the fabric. See Diagram I. Topstitch the block in place.

DIAGRAM I

2. Cut the lace into two 18" pieces. Lay the rectangle on a flat surface. Referring to the photo, position the lace along the long edges of the rectangle, aligning the edge of the lace with the top and bottom of the block. Check to make sure the lace is out of the seam area, and pin it in place. With matching thread, topstitch the lace to the cover.

3. Cover the cord with the gold moiré bias strip, using a zipper foot and a ½" seam allowance. Trim the seam allowance to ¼". With raw edges even, pin the piping around the outside edge of the cover; overlap the ends and trim the excess. Baste the piping in position.

4. Turn under ¼", then ½" along one long edge of both flap pieces; stitch the hem.

5. Place the cover face up on the batting. With raw edges matching, pin the flaps right side down on the cover; sew in place, stitching through all layers. Clip the seam allowances. Do not turn right side out.

6. Place the remaining moiré rectangle face down on the cover, with the flaps between the layers. Sew around three sides, leaving one end open. Stitch on top of or just outside the previous line of stitches. Turn the cover right side out through the open end; whipstitch the end closed. Add trims as desired.

It's easy to transfer your favorite poem to a pillow using the new photo transfer methods. Then, simply choose ribbons in colors to match and weave them into a border to sew around the fabric poem. Center the poem with the ribbon border on the front of a purchased ruffled pillow in a coordinating color and you have a first anniversary keepsake!

FIRST ANNIVERSARY SAMPLER

MATERIALS

- 10" x 12" piece of cranberry moiré fabric
- 10" x 12" piece of fleece
- Crystal and seed beads
- Embroidery floss in pink, cream, two shades of blue, and two shades of green
- Gold pearl cotton
- 12 tiny brass picture frames
- Picture frame with 7¾" x 9¾" opening
- Cardboard to fit frame
- Tacky glue

PREPARE THE EMBROIDERY

1. Using the pattern, center and stitch the embroidery onto the cranberry moiré fabric.

2. Layer the fabric and the fleece. Using matching thread, machine quilt around the embroidered center in a ¼" diagonal grid.

3. Wrap the fabric around a piece of cardboard, making sure the embroidery is centered on the front. Glue the excess fabric to the back of the cardboard.

4. Glue a tiny photo or memento into each brass picture frame. If possible, choose one to represent each month in the first year of marriage. Use the pearl cotton to tie a bow at the top of each frame. Glue the mini frames in place on the front.

5. Place the sampler in the frame, and put the backing in behind it. If necessary, put a layer or two of cardboard between the back of the sampler and the backing of the frame. This will keep the sampler from moving around within the frame.

a year of happiness

Monday's child is fair of face,
Tuesday's child is full of grace,
Wednesday's child is full of woe,
Thursday's child has far to go,
Friday's child is loving and giving,
Saturday's child works hard for his living,
And the child born on the Sabbath day,
Is bonny and blithe, and good and gay.

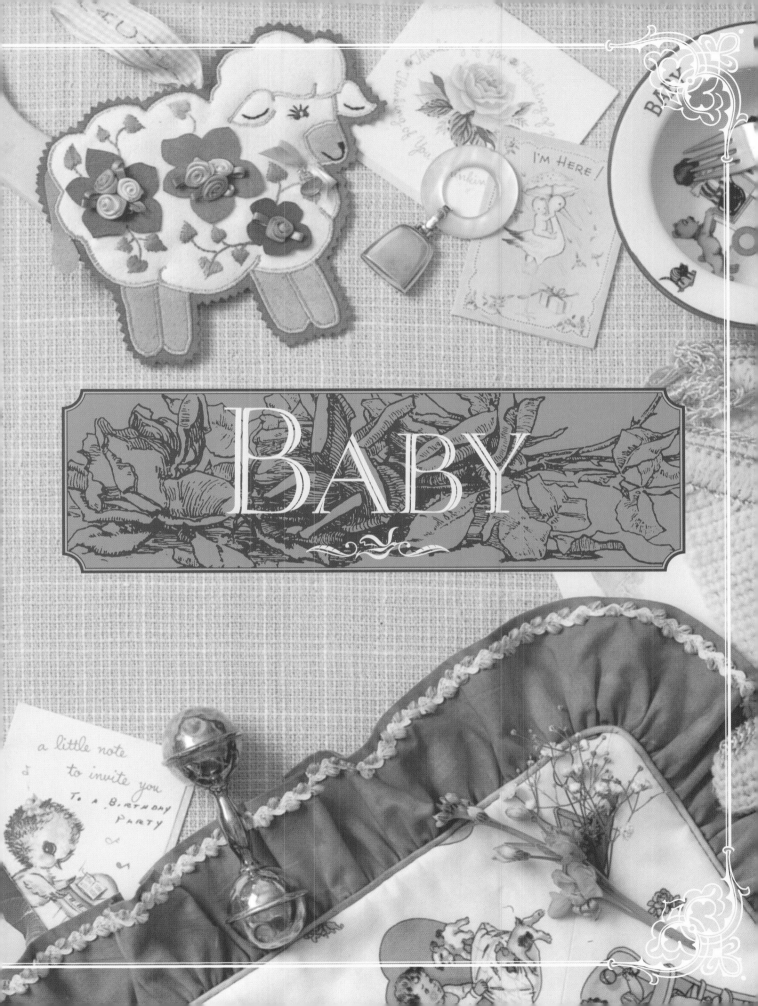

BABY

Monday's child is fair of face,
Tuesday's child is full of grace,
Wednesday's child is full of woe,
Thursday's child has far to go,
Friday's child is loving and giving,
Saturday's child works hard for his living,
And the child born on the Sabbath day,
Is bonny and blithe, and good and gay.

A New Hand In Ours

Memories of baby's first year are often those we cherish most, since the precious days of childhood are so fleeting. Quilted memories and keepsakes such as the Monday's Child quilt, Tumbling Blocks pillow, and little lamb ornament shown here become tender reminders of days gone by with the simple addition of embroidered verses, names, and other personalized accents just for baby.

Monday's child is fair of face,
Tuesday's child is full of grace,
Wednesday's child is full of woe,
Thursday's child has far to go,
Friday's child is loving and giving,
Saturday's child works hard for his living,
And the child born on the Sabbath day,
Is bonny and blithe, and good and gay.

The charming scalloped border on my birth announcement is the inspiration for the scalloped ruffles on the baby quilt and pillow.

reate memories with embroidered verses from a favorite nursery rhyme on the Monday's Child baby quilt. Use floss in a contrasting color to highlight baby's special day of the week. An accordian envelope to hold documents and keepsakes for baby can be practical as well as pretty. Simply fold a purchased placemat in thirds, stitch up the sides, add ribbon ties and trims, and fuse a fabric transfer of the birth announcement to the front flap.

For other inspirations using photo transfer paper, please turn the page.

magine how much fun and frolic you can have with our little lamb! Just the right size for an ornament, the embroidered fleece cutout can also become the centerpiece of a charming wall decor or mobile for the nursery. Use your imagination to cut simple shapes from cardboard and top them off with iron-on fabric photo transfers of your favorite "cloud kids."

Baby

Htreasured father and son photograph becomes the inspiration for A New Hand In Ours cross-stitch inset for the lid of a wooden keepsake memory box. Choose a favorite photograph of a newborn to fit an oval frame and then center it in a border of Nine-Patch blocks that works up quickly in cross-stitch.

San Diego Birth Center

A Precious Bundle, answering to,
Michael Cameron Johnston
weighing, 7 lbs. 2½ ozs.,
was delivered 4-19-80,
at the Birth Center by,
Dr. Lapp
and received by Rebecca & Peter
at 3:08 p.m.

Baby

oft blocks for baby are safe and fun. Use scraps of fabric and foam cubes to whip up a stack of blocks, each featuring as many as six iron-on fabric photo transfers—enough for everyone to get in the act. Since the photo baby blocks work up so quickly, you can treat the entire family to quilted memories by the dozen!

*Candid photographs of children are the best reminders of good times
and good fun. Stacking soft blocks for baby are a great way to keep
them smiling forever!*

MONDAY'S CHILD QUILT

31½" x 33" including ruffle

MATERIALS

- 2 yards of bright blue fabric for ruffle and back

- 1 yard of baby print fabric for outer border

- ½ yard of cream fabric for center panel

- ½ yard of hot pink fabric for inner border

- ½ yard of lime green fabric for piping

- Scraps of assorted pink fabrics for yo-yo flowers

- 25½" x 27" batting

- 3½ yards of ⅛" cording

- 6¼ yards of flat rosebud trim

- 1¾ yards of 4mm blue silk ribbon

- 2¼ yards of 7mm green silk ribbon

- Light, medium, and dark pink pearl cotton

- Pink rayon thread

- Fusible web

CUTTING

1. From the bright blue fabric, cut a 26¼" x 27¾" rectangle for the quilt back. Cut five 6¾" x 44" strips for the ruffle.

2. From the baby print fabric, cut two 5⅜" x 30½" strips and two 5⅜" x 32" strips for the borders.

3. From the cream fabric, cut a 15" x 17" rectangle for the center panel. You will trim this to size after the embroidery is complete.

4. From the hot pink fabric, cut a 16½" x 18" rectangle for the center panel.

5. From the lime green fabric, cut enough 1¼"-wide bias strips to cover the cording. Sew the strips together into one long strip.

EMBROIDER THE CENTER PANEL

1. Machine embroider the poem in the center of the cream rectangle, or take the fabric to a local custom embroidery shop (the kind of shop that makes custom T-shirts and caps) and have it stitched for you. Use a contrasting color thread to highlight the baby's day of birth.

2. Fuse the embroidered rectangle to a piece of fusible web. Making sure the embroidery is centered, trim the rectangle to 13½" x 15". Use the corner template on page 45 to trim the corners, if desired.

3. Center the embroidered rectangle on the pink rectangle, and fuse. Using the pink rayon thread, machine satin stitch around the edge of the center panel.

4. Referring to the photo, use the blue silk ribbon to sew a long running stitch just inside the edge of the center panel.

5. Use the pink fabric scraps to make 13 yo-yo flowers. To make a yo-yo flower, cut a

3¼"-diameter circle from fabric. Turn under ¼" to the wrong side, and hand-sew a line of gathering stitches around the edge. Pull the thread to gather the circle. Holding the gathered side up, use pearl cotton to make several French knots in the center of the flower.

6. Cut 6" lengths of the green ribbon and loop each into a figure 8. Center a yo-yo flower on each ribbon loop and hand-stitch them together. Referring to the photo, arrange the 13 flowers on the center panel and hand-stitch in place.

ASSEMBLE THE QUILT

1. With right sides together and using a ¼" seam allowance, sew the borders to the center panel, starting and stopping the seams ¼" away from the edge of the panel.

2. Working on one corner at a time, place one border on top of the adjacent border as shown in Diagram A. Fold the top border under so that it forms a 45-degree angle; press the fold.

Fold top border at 45° angle

3. Fold the quilt top right sides together, matching the border edges. Sew along the fold line from the corner out to the edge of the border. See Diagram B.

DIAGRAM A

4. Unfold the quilt top and check to make sure the miter is flat. Trim the seam allowance to ¼". Repeat for all four corners. Press the borders, then round the corners slightly.

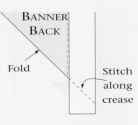

BANNER BACK

Fold

Stitch along crease

DIAGRAM B

Monday's child is fair of face
Tuesday's child is full of grace
Wednesday's child is full of woe
Thursday's child has far to go
Friday's child is loving and giving
Saturday's child works hard for a living
And the child born on the Sabbath day
Is bonny and blithe, and good and gay.

5. Using a zipper foot and a ½" seam allowance, cover the cording with the green fabric strip. Trim the seam allowance to ⅜". Baste the piping to the quilt top.

6. Sew the ruffle strips together into one long strip; stitch the ends together to make a loop. Fold in half lengthwise, wrong sides together; press. Stitch the rosebud trim about ¼" in from the folded edge.

7. Sew two rows of gathering stitches along the raw edge of the ruffle strip. Gather the ruffle to fit the quilt top; pin and baste in place on top of the piping.

8. Pin the batting to the wrong side of the quilt top. With the batting against the machine, stitch the batting and quilt top together, stitching the piping and ruffle in place at the same time. Remove the basting stitches.

9. Place the backing face down on the quilt top, with the ruffle between the layers and out of the seam area; pin. With the batting against the machine, sew the layers together with a ⅜" seam allowance, leaving a 10" opening along one side for turning. Turn right side out through the opening; hand-stitch the opening closed.

TUMBLING BLOCKS PILLOW

17" square including the ruffle

MATERIALS

- 1 yard of bright blue fabric for patchwork, ruffle, and back
- ¼ yard of dark blue fabric for patchwork
- ¼ yard of hot pink fabric for patchwork and piping
- Assorted pink fabric scraps for yo-yo flowers
- 1½ yards of ⅜"-wide pink double-faced satin ribbon
- 1 yard of 7mm green silk ribbon
- Light, medium, and dark pink pearl cotton
- 1½ yards of ⅛" cording
- 12" square pillow form

CUTTING

1. From the bright blue fabric, cut three 5¾" x 42" strips for the ruffle and one 12¾" square for the back. Using the patterns on page 43, cut nine A diamonds. Be sure to transfer the dots from the pattern to the wrong side of each fabric piece.

2. From the dark blue fabric, cut nine A diamonds, two C pieces, and two D pieces using the patterns on page 43.

3. From the hot pink fabric, cut eight A diamonds, two B pieces, two C pieces, and two D pieces. Cut enough 1¼"-wide bias strips to cover the piping cord. Sew the bias strips together into one long strip.

PIECE THE PILLOW TOP

1. Referring to Diagram C, sew the dark blue and bright blue diamonds together in strips. Start and stop the seams at the dots, backstitching at both ends. Press the seams open.

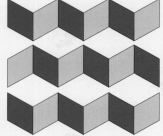

DIAGRAM C

2. Set-in the pink diamonds to complete the Tumbling Block. To set-in the pieces, place a pink diamond right sides together with a dark blue or bright blue diamond, matching the dots. Pin the pieces, and sew from dot to dot, starting at the outside edge and sewing in toward the seam between the blue diamonds. Stop with the needle down between the two blue diamonds; the needle should be in the pink fabric only. See Diagram D.

DIAGRAM D

3. With the needle down, pivot the pieces, match the adjacent side of the pink diamond to the second blue diamond, and finish sewing the seam, stopping at the dot. See Diagram E.

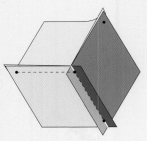

DIAGRAM E

4. Referring to Diagram F for correct placement, set-in the B, C, and D pieces to complete the pillow top.

5. Using dark pink pearl cotton make a French knot at each intersection of diamonds.

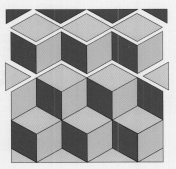

DIAGRAM F

6. Referring to Steps 5 and 6 in Embroider the Center Panel on page 36, make six yo-yo flowers from assorted pink fabric scraps, referring to the photos below. Arrange the yo-yos and ribbon loops on the pillow top as desired, and hand-stitch in place.

ASSEMBLE THE PILLOW

1. Using a zipper foot and a ½" seam allowance, cover the cord with the pink strip. Trim the seam allowance to ⅜". Baste the piping in place around the edge of the pillow top.

2. Sew the ruffle strips together into one long strip; sew the ends together to make a loop. Fold the strip in half lengthwise, wrong sides together; press. Sew two rows of gathering stitches along the raw edge of the ruffle fabric.

3. Divide the ruffle into quarters and mark. Pin the quarter points to the corners of the pillow top, and gather the ruffle to fit. Pin, then baste the ruffle in place on top of the piping.

4. Place the pillow back face down on the pieced top, with the ruffle between the layers and out of the seam area. Stitch with a ⅜" seam allowance, leaving an opening along one side for turning and stuffing.

5. Turn right side out through the opening. Insert the pillow form, and stitch the opening closed.

6. Cut the pink satin ribbon into two equal lengths. Tie a small knot in each end of both ribbons. Place one ribbon on top of the other, and hand-tack the center of the ribbons to the center of the pillow. Tie a teething ring in the ribbons as shown in the photo.

OUR LITTLE LAMB ORNAMENT

6" x 6⅜"

MATERIALS

- Scraps of teal green, white, light pink, hot pink, purple, and dark purple Ultrasuede

- 5" x 7" piece of fleece

- ⅜ yard of ⅞"-wide green check ribbon

- 4" length of ¼"-wide green satin ribbon or small purchased bow

- Seven purchased ribbon roses

- Green, yellow-green, pink, black, and blue embroidery floss

- Pink rayon thread

- Fusible web

- ½" gold bell charm

ASSEMBLY

1. Trace the lamb pattern on page 44 onto the paper side of fusible web, tracing the legs, tail, and nose separately. The pattern is printed in reverse so that it is facing the right way in the finished project. Trace the three flower shapes. Cut out the pieces, cutting just beyond the traced lines.

2. Fuse the body to white Ultrasuede; fuse the legs, tail, and nose to pink Ultrasuede; and fuse the flowers to pink and purple Ultrasuede as shown. Be sure to use a press cloth when fusing the Ultrasuede. Cut out the pieces on the traced lines.

3. Embroider an eye with blue floss, and add eyelashes and ear details with black floss. Make a French knot in the center of the eye with white floss or thread. Embroider the stems and leaves with the two shades of green floss.

4. Place the lamb body on a piece of fleece, and cut the fleece to match the pattern shape. Then, trim the fleece so that it is about ⅛" smaller than the Ultrasuede shape. Fuse the fleece to the Ultrasuede lamb.

5. Position the body, legs, tail, and nose on a slightly oversized piece of teal green Ultrasuede, referring to the photo and the pattern for proper placement. Pin the body in place, then fuse the other pieces around it. Using the pink rayon thread, machine satin stitch around the pieces, adding details as indicated by the dashed lines on the pattern. Do not stitch down the end of the tail.

6. Use pinking shears to cut out the green Ultrasuede, cutting about ⅛" beyond the edge of the lamb shape.

7. Hand-sew or glue the ribbon roses to the flowers as desired. Hand-sew or glue the flowers to the lamb. Use black embroidery floss to add details to the lamb's nose. Make a tiny bow with the ¼"-wide green ribbon, and stitch the bow and the bell just below the lamb's nose.

8. Lightly mark the baby's name on one end of the green check ribbon. Hand-embroider the name using a backstitch. Fold the ribbon in half with the name facing front, and stitch to the upper back of the ornament. Trim excess ribbon as desired.

A New Hand in Ours
Keepsake Box

MATERIALS

- 8" x 10" piece of 32-count blue cross-stitch fabric

- Large scraps of felt or Ultrasuede (optional)

- Yellow, orange, aqua, pink, purple, yellow-green, and mint green embroidery floss

- 6¼" x 8¼" wooden box with a lid designed to accept needlework*

- Four ⅜" gold cushion beads

- Photo of baby

- 3" x 4" oval photo frame

- Gold photo transfer paper*

- 1¾" gold key charm

- 3" x 4" cardboard or mat board

The box shown is the Picture Frame Box by Sudberry House. The transfer paper is from Janlynn Cre8 ComputerCrafts. See Sources for details.

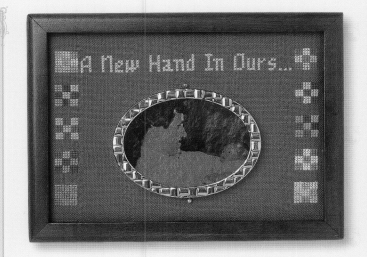

ASSEMBLY

1. Referring to the chart on page 45, work the cross stitch over two threads using two strands of floss. Work the letters in yellow, and the Nine-Patch blocks in assorted colors as desired.

2. Center the design on the mounting board, and reassemble the lid according to the manufacturer's instructions. If desired, line the lid and the inside of the box with felt or Ultrasuede, cutting pieces to size and gluing them in place.

3. To create the framed photo, first scan the photo into the computer. Using a color inkjet printer and following the manufacturer's instructions, print the image onto gold paper. Cut out the photo, and glue it to the cardboard or mat board. You could also use an actual photo in the frame; simply glue the photo to cardboard and trim as directed.

4. Take apart the small oval frame, removing the backing. Cut the mounted photo to the shape of the backing. Reassemble the frame with the photo inside, and glue it to the center of the box lid.

5. Glue the gold cushion beads to the bottom of the box at the corners. Tie several strands of floss to the top of the key charm, and glue the charm to the front of the box.

BABY BLOCKS

MATERIALS

For three blocks:

- ⅛ yard each or large scraps of the following fabrics: blue-and-yellow plaid, green-and-pink plaid, blue check, blue print, green print, and pink print

- 8" square of muslin

- Blue, yellow, light pink, dark pink, light green, and dark green pearl cotton

- Three 4¼" x 4¼" x 4¼" foam cubes

- Photo transfer paper for color laser copiers*

*The paper used in this project is Creative Copy™ Photo Transfer Paper by Quiltmakers. See Sources for details.

CUTTING

1. From the blue-and-yellow plaid, green-and-pink plaid, and blue check fabrics, cut five 3½" squares each.

2. From the blue, green, and pink print fabrics, cut twelve 3" squares each. Cut each square in half diagonally.

ASSEMBLY

1. Following the manufacturer's instructions, transfer three 3" square photo images onto the muslin square. Be sure to leave at least ½" between the images. Cut the muslin into 3½" squares.

2. Sew a print triangle to opposite sides of each photo transfer square; press. Sew triangles to the two remaining sides of each square, and press. See Diagram G.

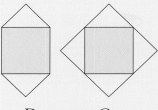

DIAGRAM G

3. In the same manner, sew coordinating print triangles to each plaid square; press.

4. Sew three pieced squares and a photo square together in a strip, as shown in Diagram H. Bring the edges of the first and last squares right sides together and sew, forming a loop.

5. With right sides together, pin a matching square to one end of the loop. Stitch the square to the loop, creating the bottom of the block. For best results, stop stitching each seam ¼" from the corner, lower the needle into the fabric, pivot the fabric, and stitch the next side.

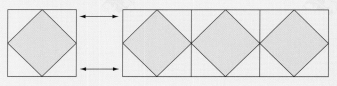

DIAGRAM H

6. In the same manner, pin the remaining square to the opposite end of the block. Stitch two adjacent sides only at this time.

7. Turn the block right side out. Insert a foam cube into the block, and whipstitch the last two sides closed.

8. Thread a needle with two different colors of pearl cotton. Take a single stitch at the mid-point of each edge, at the corners of the plaid squares. Tie a double knot and clip the threads, leaving ½" tails.

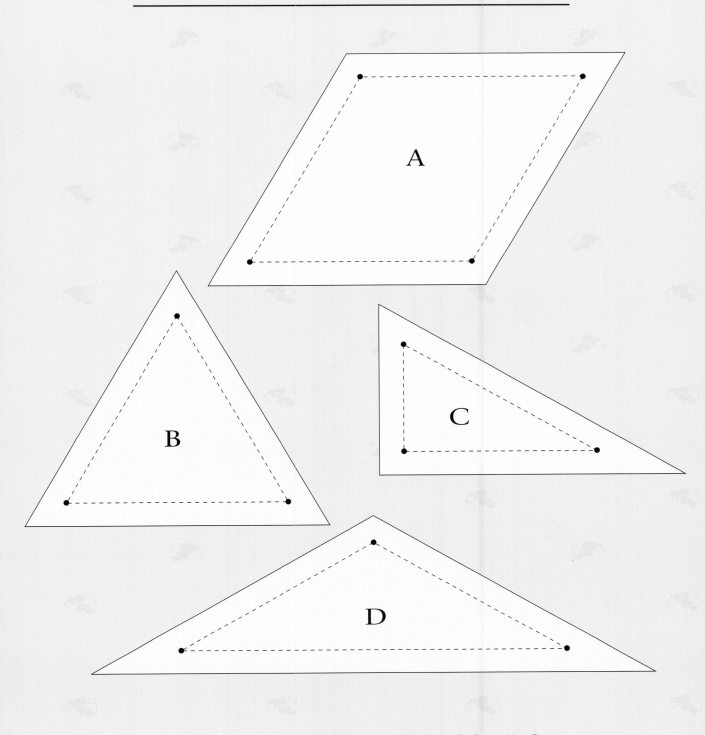

OUR LITTLE LAMB ORNAMENT

CORNER TEMPLATE

Sarah Lyn
Ankeny High School

GRADUATION

Reach for the Stars

Graduation is a time for looking forward to the future with anticipation and high hopes. The old adage, "Those who reach, touch the stars," certainly applies to this exciting season of great expectations. Here and on the following pages, you'll find a memorable awards banner and a fabulous collection of graduation party projects and ideas to celebrate your graduate's success with personal style.

Autographs have long been a way to express heartfelt sentiments that might otherwise go unsaid.

School colors and symbols set the scene for an autograph pillow and an unusual photo frame inspired by academic and athletic award letters. Choose a fun photo featuring the graduate's favorite extra-curricular activity. The costumed student's flair for drama is obvious in the letter photo shown below.

hether off to college or a career, the graduate can take along fond memories of team spirit with a patchwork laundry bag. Logo T-shirts from high school are the basis for quilt blocks quick-sashed with grosgrain ribbons and trimmed with buttons.

Generously sized to handle a load of laundry, the bag is sure to be a terrific conversation piece as well!

Awards Banner

25" x 31"

MATERIALS

- 1½ yards of cream fabric for center panel and back

- 1 yard of contrasting fabric for sashing and binding

- ½ yard of print fabric for leaf appliqués

- Large scrap of muslin

- 29" x 35" thin quilt batting

- Gold metallic thread

- Thread to match the appliqués

- 4 yards of narrow, flat gold braid for trim and hanger

- Photo and school logo

- Iron-on fabric sheets*

- Fusible web

- Awards for trim

- ⅜" wooden dowel (optional)

*This project was made with Janlynn Cre8 ComputerCrafts sheets. See Sources for details.

GRADUATION

The projects in this chapter feature computer-generated images printed onto special iron-on fabric sheets. To use the sheets, you must have access to a scanner and a color ink-jet printer (not a laser printer or photocopier). You could also make any of the projects using photo transfer paper.

APPLIQUÉ THE CENTER PANEL

1. To prepare the computer-generated appliqués, first scan the logo and the photo into the computer. Using a color ink-jet printer and following the manufacturer's instructions, print the images onto the iron-on fabric sheets. Print the student's name and the name of the school onto an iron-on sheet. Cut out the appliqués.

2. Fuse each appliqué to a slightly oversized piece of muslin. Cut the muslin ⅛" beyond the edge of the appliqué.

3. To make the leaf appliqués, trace the pattern on page 59, matching A to B to make the complete pattern. Trace onto the paper side of a piece of fusible web; flip the pattern over and trace a second leaf in reverse. Loosely cut out

around the shapes. Fuse to the wrong side of the print fabric. Cut out the appliqués on the drawn lines.

4. Cut a 17" x 23" rectangle from the cream fabric. Arrange all the appliqués on the center panel as desired. Fuse, then machine appliqué the leaves. Machine appliqué the remaining pieces, stitching on the muslin, not on the iron-on sheet.

ADD THE BORDERS

1. From the contrasting fabric, cut two strips 4½" x 30" and two strips 4½" x 36".

2. With right sides together and using a ¼" seam allowance, sew the borders to the center panel, starting and stopping the seams ¼" away from the edge of the panel.

3. Working on one corner at a time, place one border on top of the adjacent border as shown in Diagram A. Fold the top border under so that it forms a 45-degree angle; press the fold.

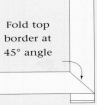

Fold top border at 45° angle

DIAGRAM A

4. Fold the banner right sides together, matching the border edges. Sew along the fold line from the banner corner out to the edge of the border. See Diagram B.

5. Unfold the banner and check to make sure the miter is flat. Trim the seam allowance to ¼".

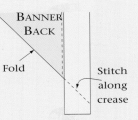

BANNER BACK

Fold

Stitch along crease

DIAGRAM B

FINISH THE BANNER

1. From the cream fabric, cut a 25" x 31" backing piece. From the contrasting fabric, cut three 2" x 44" binding strips.

2. Layer the top, batting, and backing. Pin the layers securely. Machine quilt around the appliqués and in the ditch between the center panel and the borders.

3. Sew the binding strips end to end into one long strip. Fold in half lengthwise, wrong sides together; press. With raw edges even, stitch the binding to the front of the quilt, mitering the corners. Bring the folded edge to the back and whipstitch in place.

4. Hot-glue the gold braid around the edges along the binding seam. Make a hanger from the remaining length of braid by gluing or hand-stitching the ends of the braid to the top back of the banner. If you have numerous or somewhat heavy awards, you may wish to add a hanging sleeve and a dowel for extra support. Cut a strip of backing fabric 4" x 24". On each short end, turn under ¼", then ¼" again; press, then stitch to hem. Fold the strip in half lengthwise, right sides together, and sew with a ¼" seam allowance. Turn the tube right side out, center the seam on one side, and press. Center the sleeve, seam side down, on the top back of the banner; whipstitch along both long sides. Insert a ⅜" dowel trimmed to length.

5. Decorate the banner as desired with letters, ribbons, pins, and other awards.

AUTOGRAPH PILLOW

15½" x 20" including ruffle

MATERIALS

- ⅓ yard of cream fabric for pillow front
- ⅓ yard of cotton batiste for lining
- 1 yard of contrasting fabric for ruffle and backing
- 12" x 18" piece of thin quilt batting
- Scrap of muslin
- 2 yards of narrow sew-in gold piping
- Matching thread
- Polyester stuffing
- School logo for appliqué
- Iron-on fabric sheet*
- Fusible web
- Permanent fabric marking pens

*This project was made with Janlynn Cre8 ComputerCrafts sheets. See Sources for details.

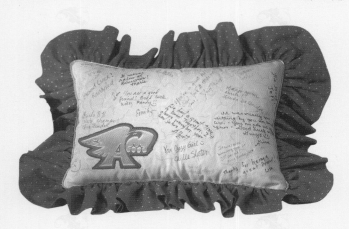

PREPARE THE PILLOW FRONT

1. Cut a 12" x 18" piece of cream fabric for the pillow front. Cut a 12" x 18" piece of cotton batiste for the front lining.

2. Scan the school logo into the computer. Using a color ink-jet printer and following the manufacturer's instructions, print it onto the iron-on fabric sheet. Cut out the logo.

3. Fuse the logo to a slightly oversized piece of muslin. Cut the muslin ⅛" beyond the edge of the logo. Position the logo on the pillow front and machine appliqué in place, stitching on the muslin, not on the iron-on sheet. Use matching thread.

4. Layer the pillow front with the batting and batiste; pin baste. Machine quilt as desired. Trim the pillow front to 10" x 14½", cutting through all layers.

ASSEMBLE THE PILLOW

1. Pin the sew-in piping to the right side of the pillow front, matching raw edges. Stitch.

2. From the ruffle fabric, cut three 6¾" x 44" strips. Join the strips end to end to make one strip 94" long. Sew the ends together, creating a loop.

3. Fold the ruffle loop in half lengthwise, wrong sides together; press. Sew a row of gathering stitches along the raw edge. Gather the ruffle to fit the pillow front. Matching the raw edges, pin the ruffle to the right side of the pillow front on top of the piping. Stitch using a ¼" seam allowance.

FINISH THE PILLOW

1. Cut a 10" x 14½" piece for the pillow back.

2. Place the pillow front face down on the back, with the ruffle between the layers and out of the seam area. Stitch, leaving an opening for turning. Trim the seam allowance, and turn right side out.

3. Stuff the pillow firmly. Sew the opening closed.

4. Have friends autograph with permanent markers.

SCHOOL LETTER PICTURE FRAME

8½" x 8½"

MATERIALS

- 10" square each of two colors of Ultrasuede

- 10" square of foamcore

- 10" square mat board

- Tacky fabric glue

- Craft knife

- Iron-on fabric sheet*

*This project was made with Janlynn Cre8 ComputerCrafts sheets. See Sources for details.

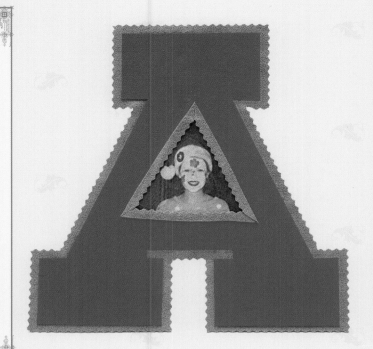

ASSEMBLE THE FRAME

1. Make a paper pattern for the appropriate school letter. There are several ways to do this: trace an actual school letter onto paper; scan a letter into a computer and print out a pattern; or trace a letter from a book (a child's alphabet book or coloring book is a good source). Enlarge the pattern to desired size and cut out.

2. Trace the letter onto the foamcore and carefully cut it out using a craft knife.

3. Apply glue to the front of the foamcore letter, and center it face down on one piece of Ultrasuede. Cut with pinking shears ¼" outside the foamcore letter.

4. Trace the letter pattern onto the second piece of Ultrasuede, and cut it out. Center and glue the second letter on top of the first, larger letter.

5. Scan the photo into the computer. Using a color ink-jet printer and following the manufacturer's instructions, print the photo onto the iron-on fabric sheet. Cut out the printed photo. If you prefer, use photo transfer paper or use an actual photo.

6. Trim the photo to fit an appropriate space on the letter. If the letter has an opening, such as the A shown in the photo, or a B, D, or R, trim the photo to fit the opening. For letters with horizontal or vertical lines, such as E, H, L, T, determine the photo's placement and trim to fit.

7. Glue the photo to the front of the frame. Use pinking shears to cut ¼" strips of Ultrasuede for the photo border. Glue the strips around the photo.

8. To make an easel, cut a piece of mat board 1½" wide. Mark a line 1" down from the top. Score the board along the line, being careful not to cut all the way through the mat. Fold on the score line. Glue the top, above the fold line, to the back of the letter.

T-SHIRT QUILT BLOCKS LAUNDRY BAG

29" x 32"

MATERIALS

- 2 yards of bag fabric
- 2 yards of lining fabric
- 6 T-shirts with logos
- 6 yards of 1½"-wide grosgrain ribbon
- 100 assorted buttons
- Pearl cotton to attach buttons
- Fusible interfacing
- 2 yards of cord for drawstring
- Two 1" wooden beads with large hole

PREPARE THE T-SHIRTS

1. Cut the T-shirt logos from the shirts. For best results, cut all shirt panels the same width; plan the layout so that the lengths are the same on the left and right sides. (The appliquéd area on the bag shown measures 29" wide and 26" long.)

2. Fuse the interfacing to the wrong side of the T-shirt panels.

ASSEMBLE THE BAG FRONT

1. Cut two bag pieces 30¼" x 39". Cut two linings 30¼" wide and 27" long.

2. Arrange the T-shirts on the right side of one bag piece, making sure the outside edges of the T-shirt panels are at least 1¼" from the

side and bottom edges of the bag and approximately 13" from the top edge. Baste the T-shirts to the bag. See Diagram C. To make the pocket, place a piece of bag fabric wrong sides together with one of the T-shirt panels; baste around the edges. Fold a piece of ribbon over the top edge; topstitch in place. Baste the pocket in place on the bag.

3. Cut strips of ribbon and topstitch in place to cover the basting.

FINISH THE BAG

1. Place the bag front and back right sides together. Sew the sides and bottom together using a ⅝" seam allowance. Sew the two lining pieces right sides together using a ⅝" seam allowance.

2. Turn the bag inside out and the lining right side out. Place the lining inside the bag and sew the two together around the top edge, leaving an opening for turning. Turn right side out through the opening; stitch the opening closed.

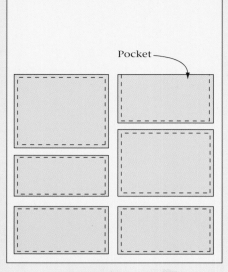

DIAGRAM C

3. Tuck the lining inside the bag. Since the lining is shorter than the bag, the top of the bag will fold over to the inside about 6". Smooth the lining inside the bag, and press the fold at the top edge.

4. Sew a line of stitches 2" from the top folded edge of the bag. Sew a second line of stitches 1¼" below the first to make the casing for the drawstring.

5. Open the casing at the side seam, and pull the cord through the casing. Put beads on the ends of the cord.

6. Using pearl cotton, sew buttons on the ribbons as desired. Stack buttons in contrasting colors for added effect.

CUT 1
AND
1 REVERSE

GRADUATION BANNER
LEAF APPLIQUÉ

One H
One Heart

WEDDING

From This Day Forward

From the first magical moments of the proposal to the tossing of the bridal bouquet, hearts and flowers speak the language of love. Discover the joy of creating a treasury of quilted memories starting with the bride's friendship bouquet quilt shown here and on the following pages. You'll also find a romantic heart-shaped crazy-quilt bridal bag and other wedding keepsakes sure to become cherished remembrances of the bride's special day.

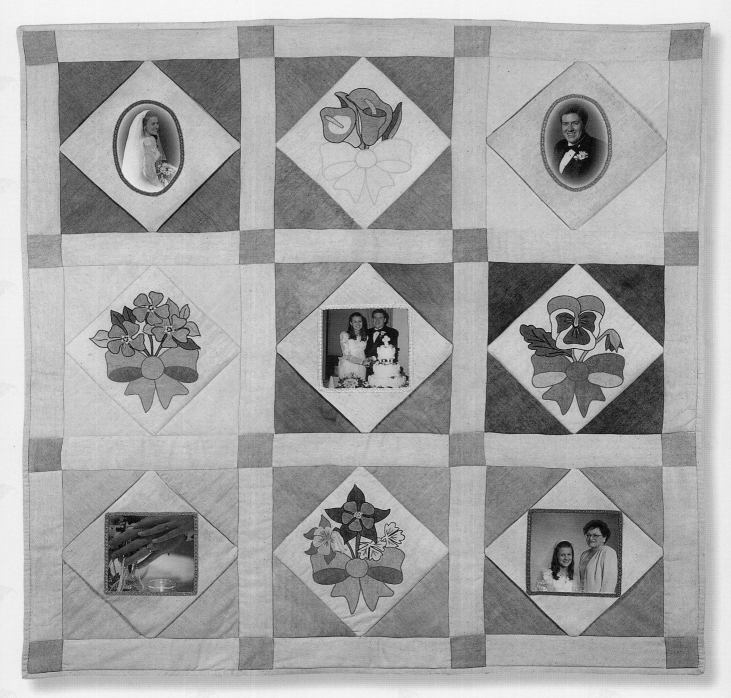

For me, fresh-picked flowers from the garden have

been a favorite source of inspiration for the many

quilts I've designed over the years.

reating quilted memories for the wedding begins at the bridal shower when you surprise the bride with personalized message buttons prepared in advance by the guests (see page 74). Later, display these embroidered sentiments on the bride's friendship quilt.

After the wedding, mix and match iron-on transfers of favorite photographs of the bride and groom with the fresh floral appliqués for the quilt blocks. Tie it all together with the blue bow repeated on each of the everlasting bouquets (there are nine to choose from!) and finish it off with a matching ruffled pillow.

avished with lace and ribbon flowers, the bride's card box and heart-trio photo frame take center stage on the guest table at the wedding. A graceful addition to the guest book, the lace-trimmed card box is actually a purchased sewing basket the bride can use later for sewing supplies.

Crowning glory for the box lid is a cluster of silk ribbon flowers, which can also serve as inspiration for a ribbon corsage for the mother or grandmother of the bride.

Instructions for transforming the sewing basket into the bride's card box and for making the ribbon corsage begin on page 76.

I love to dream up elegant accent pieces like the bride's card

box that will also serve a practical purpose for years to come.

n keeping with the Victorians' love affair with crazy-quilting scraps of satin, silk, moiré taffeta, and velvet, this richly embellished crazy-quilt bridal bag is the perfect place to carry "something old, new, borrowed, and blue." Open the bridal bag and one heart becomes two, with pockets for the bride's jewelry and other special keepsakes—to have and to hold from this day forward!

 petite purse stitched from Grandmother's hankies and made new to look old, truly fits all the criteria of "something old, new, borrowed and blue." Shown opposite, antique hankies are the basis for the tassel-trimmed bag topped by a 5" purchased silver purse handle.

Keepsakes from my own wedding—the gown, gloves, and satin-bow trimmed shoes—are the backdrop for the bride's hankie trimmed with a blue appliqué bow and ribbon. Thanks to easy fusible appliqué, the bride will have a keepsake hankie with something blue in no time at all!

For something new, personalize a ceramic ring box with an iron-on fabric transfer of a romantic antique greeting.

To me, preserving the past for the future is important. My home is filled with family heirlooms, including a prized collection of antique linens and hankies.

BRIDE'S FRIENDSHIP BOUQUET QUILT

Quilt is 56¼" square

MATERIALS

- 2¾ yards of peach fabric for blocks, sashing, and binding

- ½ yard each of the following fabrics for blocks and appliqués: yellow; mint green; medium rose; light and medium purple; light, medium, and dark pink; light, medium, and dark blue

- ¼ yard each of light and medium sage green fabric for appliqués

- 3½ yards of 44-45" fabric or 2 yards of 60"-wide fabric for back

- 60" square batting

- Matching and contrasting thread

- Matching and contrasting embroidery floss

- Transparent nylon thread

- Fusible web

- Sixteen 2½" half-ball button forms

CUTTING

1. From the peach fabric, cut nine 11" squares and twenty-four 3½" x 15¼" sashing strips. Cut six 3" x 44" binding strips to make a ⅝" double-fold binding.

2. From the light blue, medium blue, light purple, medium purple, medium pink, dark pink, and rose fabrics, cut two 8¼" squares each. From the yellow fabric, cut four 8¼" squares. Cut each square in half diagonally.

3. From the mint green fabric, cut sixteen 3½" corner squares.

APPLIQUÉ THE BLOCKS

1. Trace the flowers, stems, leaves, and bow from the patterns on pages 82-91. You'll need to trace the patterns in reverse in order to have them facing the right way in the block. Using a pencil, trace onto the web side of the fusible web, then turn it over and darken the lines on the paper side. Use a light box or hold the pattern against a window to make it easier to redraw the pattern on the paper side. Following the manufacturer's instructions and using the photo as a guide to color placement, fuse the appliqué patterns to the wrong side of the fabrics.

2. Cut out the appliqués and fuse them to the peach background squares, overlapping the pieces as indicated by the dashed lines on the patterns. For best results, position all the pieces in a block and check their placement before fusing.

3. Machine appliqué or satin stitch around each petal, stem, leaf, and bow shape with matching or contrasting thread. Detail the flower centers and leaves with French knots, straight stitch, and backstitch, referring to the photo and the patterns for color and placement guidance.

ASSEMBLE THE QUILT TOP

1. Sew a triangle to two opposite sides of a block as shown in Diagram A; press. Sew triangles to the two remaining sides; press. Repeat for the remaining eight blocks.

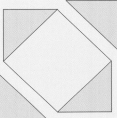

DIAGRAM A

2. Arrange the blocks in three rows of three blocks each, with the sashing strips and corner squares between them. Referring to the diagram, sew four corner squares and three sashing strips together in one vertical row; repeat for three more rows. Sew the blocks and remaining sashing strips into rows as shown. Sew the rows together.

3. Layer the backing, batting, and pieced top; baste. Machine quilt in the ditch using transparent nylon thread. Do not trim the batting and backing until the binding has been added.

4. Join the binding strips end to end to make one strip approximately 235" (6½ yards) long. Fold the strip in half lengthwise, wrong sides together, and press. Pin the binding to the quilt top, matching the raw edges. Beginning in the middle of one side, sew the binding to the quilt using a ¼" seam allowance. To miter the corners, stop sewing ¼" from the corner and remove the quilt from the machine. Fold the binding up at a 45-degree angle, then down at a 90-degree angle, and resume sewing down the next side. Sew all four corners in the same manner.

5. Trim the batting and backing to a generous ⅜" beyond the edge of the quilt top. Turn the binding to the back so that it just covers the stitching. Whipstitch the folded edge, making mitered corners on the back.

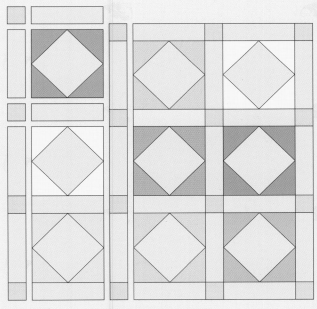

DIAGRAM B

PREPARE THE MESSAGE BUTTONS

1. To complement the gift to the bride, accent the quilt with message buttons prepared by the bridal party or shower guests. Before the event, give each guest a 4" square or circle of mint green fabric. On the wrong side of each fabric piece, lightly mark a 2½" circle; the message must fit within this circle. Have each guest embroider a message on the right side of the fabric and return it to you. Or, have the guests lightly write the message in their own hand, then embroider it for them.

2. To assemble a button, remove the backing from a half-ball button form. Center the design on the front, and gently pull the fabric smooth and taut as you wrap it around the form and hook it over the gripper teeth on the back side. Snap the back of the button in place. Hand stitch a button at each corner square on the quilt.

CONEFLOWER PILLOW

Pillow is 19" square, including ruffle

MATERIALS

- 1 yard of peach fabric for block, ruffle, and back
- ⅜ yard of yellow fabric for block
- ⅜ yard of medium pink fabric for piping and appliqués
- 15" square of white cotton fabric for lining
- Scraps of dark pink, light pink, medium sage green, dark blue, and light blue fabrics for appliqués
- 15" square of thin batting
- 4¼ yards of ⅛" piping
- 1¾ yards of ¼" piping
- Matching and contrasting threads
- Gold, pink, and green embroidery floss
- Fusible web
- 16" pillow form

CUTTING

1. From the peach fabric, cut one 11" square and one 15¼" square. Cut three 4½" x 44" strips for the ruffle.

2. From the yellow fabric, cut two 8¼" squares; cut the squares in half diagonally.

3. From the medium pink fabric, cut enough 1½"-wide bias strips to cover the ¼" piping.

APPLIQUÉ THE PILLOW FRONT

1. Referring to the instructions for the quilt blocks on pages 72-73, trace and fuse the coneflower appliqué patterns from page 88 onto the peach background square. Be sure to trace the patterns in reverse so that they face the right way in the finished block.

2. Machine appliqué or satin stitch around each petal, stem, leaf, and bow shape with matching or contrasting thread. Detail the flower centers with French knots.

3. Sew yellow triangles to opposite corners of the block; press. Sew the remaining triangles to the other two corners; press.

4. Layer the pillow top with the batting and the white cotton square. Hand or machine quilt around the outline of the appliqués and around the outside edge of the peach background block.

ASSEMBLE THE PILLOW

1. Sew the 1½"-wide bias strips together end to end. Cover the ¼" piping with the strip, using a zipper foot and matching thread. Trim the seam allowance to ¼".

2. With raw edges matching, pin the piping to the pillow top; baste.

3. Sew the three ruffle strips together end to end to make one long strip. Sew the short ends together, making a loop. Fold the ruffle strip in half lengthwise, wrong sides together; press lightly. Open up the strip and place the ⅛" piping in the crease. Fold the fabric over the piping. Using a zipper foot, stitch alongside the piping, making sure it stays tucked tight against the fabric. Overlap the ends of the piping slightly, and trim any excess.

4. Sew two rows of gathering stitches along the raw edge of the ruffle fabric. Divide the ruffle into quarters and mark. Pin the quarter points to the corners of the pillow top, and gather the ruffle to fit. Pin the ruffle in place on top of the piping; baste.

5. Pin the top and the back right sides together, with the ruffle between the layers and out of the seam area. Stitch with a ¼" seam allowance, leaving a large opening for turning.

6. Turn the pillow right side out through the opening, and insert the pillow form. The pillow form is intentionally larger than the cover, so you'll need to really stuff the pillow into it. The end result—an especially full and puffy pillow—is worth the extra effort. Slip-stitch the opening closed.

Special wedding photographs translate beautifully into fabric for a truly memorable wedding quilt.

BRIDE'S CARD BOX AND RIBBON CORSAGE

MATERIALS

- 1 yard of white or cream polished cotton fabric to cover sewing basket

- Approximately 1 yard of bridal lace to cover basket

- 1 yard of ⅜"-wide white double-faced satin ribbon

- 1½ yards of 2½"-wide silk ribbon for large rose

- ¾ yard each of three different 2½"-wide silk ribbons for flowers

- ¼ yard of 2½"-wide green silk ribbon for leaves

- Purchased flower stamens

- Purchased leaves

- Scrap of white felt

- Scrap of buckram

- Wooden or wicker sewing basket with handle*

- Fabric glue

  The basket shown is from Prym-Dritz Corporation. See Sources for details.

COVER THE BASKET

1. Measure the sides and top of the sewing basket, and cut pieces of the white fabric to fit. Allow enough extra on each piece to turn under the raw edges.

2. Use the fabric glue to attach the fabric to the sewing basket. You may need to cut around the basket handle on the side pieces.

3. Cut pieces of the bridal lace to fit the top and sides of the basket. Carefully glue it in place on top of the white fabric.

4. Wrap the handle in the satin ribbon, securing it with glue at each end.

MAKE THE RIBBON CORSAGE

1. The ribbon flowers on the corsage shown include a large rose, one five-petal flower (yellow), and two four-petal flowers (one blue and one small purple flower). Follow the instructions below to make an assortment of flowers as desired.

2. To make the rose, fold the ribbon in half lengthwise (use the entire 1½ yard piece). Begin by folding the right end down as shown in Diagram C. Roll the ribbon from the right edge several times.

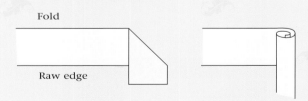

Fold

Raw edge

DIAGRAM C

3. Fold the ribbon the opposite way, and roll it twice. See Diagram D. Fold the ribbon a third time, so that

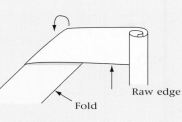

DIAGRAM D

the folded edge is once again at the top, and roll it several times. Holding the rolled center, secure it to a piece of buckram with a few stitches, leaving the rest of the ribbon hanging loose.

4. Sew a row of gathering stitches along the raw edge of the remaining length of ribbon. Gather the ribbon and wrap it around the flower center, securing it to the buckram in several places. Trim the excess buckram. Glue or stitch a stamen to the flower center.

5. To make the five-petal flower, cut a 23½" length of 2½"-wide ribbon. Fold the ribbon in half lengthwise. Lightly mark the folded edge of the ribbon at 4½" intervals as shown in Diagram E, starting ½" in from one end.

DIAGRAM E

6. Referring to the diagram, sew gathering stitches along the length of the ribbon, taking the top stitch up and over the fold each time. Gather the ribbon and join the petals in a tight circle.

7. Stitch the center to a piece of buckram. Glue or stitch a stamen to the center. Trim the excess buckram.

8. The four-petal flowers are made in the same manner as the five-petal flower. To make the larger four-petal flower, cut a 21" length of 2½"-wide ribbon. Fold the ribbon and mark it at 5" intervals, beginning ½" from one end. Stitch and gather as previously. For the small four-petal flower, cut an 11" length of ribbon, and mark it at 2½" intervals.

9. To make the leaves, cut a 2" x 2½" piece of ribbon for each leaf. Fold the ribbon right sides together, and stitch as shown in Diagram F. Turn the leaf right side out, gather the lower edge, and stitch to a flower.

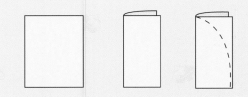

DIAGRAM F

10. Arrange the flowers as desired on a piece of white felt, filling in the background with purchased leaves. Glue the flowers and leaves in place, then trim any excess felt. Pin the ribbon corsage to the lid of the covered sewing basket, and the bride will have a beautiful card box to grace the table at her wedding reception.

It's easy to dress up a purchased photo frame with tea-dyed bridal lace and tiny ribbon roses.

CRAZY QUILT BRIDAL BAG

MATERIALS

- ½ yard of cream moiré taffeta for bag

- ½ yard of white cotton fabric for patchwork foundation

- Assorted scraps of white and cream satin, silk, moiré, velvet, and lace fabrics

- 1 yard of 1"-wide white lace trim

- Assorted scraps of white and cream lace and lace trims

- 1 yard of ¼"-wide white velvet ribbon for ties

- 1 yard of ⅜"-wide white satin ribbon for ribbon flowers

- White, cream, gold, pale yellow, and pale pink embroidery floss

- Gold thread

- Assorted small white beads

PREPARE THE PIECES

1. Trace the bag pattern on page 92 onto a folded piece of moiré; cut on the traced lines.

2. Trace the bag pattern onto a folded piece of white fabric; cut 2" outside the traced lines. Using a dark-colored thread, machine-baste along the traced lines.

3. Trim the pattern along the dashed line to make the pocket pattern. Use the trimmed pattern to trace and cut two pocket pieces from the moiré. Be sure to place the pattern on the fold of the fabric.

PIECE THE BAG FRONT

1. Cut a five-sided piece from one of the white or cream fabric scraps. Pin the shape right side up on the white base fabric, near the center of the pattern. See Diagram G. Referring to the diagram, place a second piece right side down on the first, and stitch using a ¼" seam allowance. Press the piece open.

DIAGRAM G

2. Sew a third piece to an adjacent edge, covering the edges of the first and second pieces. Trim excess seam allowance if necessary. Working in a general clockwise direction, continue to add pieces to the base until the entire pattern shape is covered.

3. Turn the base over to the back side and machine-baste again along the lines of the pattern, so that the shape is marked on the pieced side. Cut out the shape, trimming just beyond the basting stitches.

4. Referring to the photo, embroider the bag front as desired, adding bits of lace, ribbons, and charms along with the decorative stitches.

ASSEMBLE THE BAG

1. Using the photo as a guide to placement, lightly write the words "Something old, new, borrowed & blue" along the top edge of one of the pocket pieces. Check to make sure the tops of the letters are at least ½" in from the top edge to allow for the ¼" seam allowance. Stitch the words using gold embroidery floss.

2. Place the two pocket pieces right sides together and stitch along the curved edge. Turn right side out. Place the pocket right side up on the moiré lining piece, aligning the straight edges; baste. See Diagram H. Topstitch three lines to make pockets.

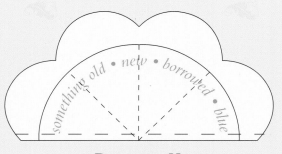

DIAGRAM H

3. Position the lace trim around the outside edge of the moiré lining piece; baste. Place the pieced front and the lining right sides together; pin. Sew with a ¼" seam allowance,

leaving an opening for turning. Turn right side out and slip-stitch the opening closed.

4. Cut the ¼"-wide velvet ribbon into two 18" pieces for ties. Referring to the photo, tack one ribbon to each side of the bag.

5. Use the ⅝"-wide ribbon to make flowers for the ends of the ties. Cut seven 2" pieces of ribbon for each flower. Have a threaded needle ready. Referring to Diagram I, fold the top end of the ribbon down and across the bottom. Fold the ribbon again, bringing the top end down behind and even with the bottom. Pinch the ends together into a pleat, and secure with a small stitch or two. Make six more flower petals in the same way. Hand-stitch seven petals together in the center. Repeat to make a second flower.

6. Sew six small white beads to the center of each flower; sew a flower to end of each tie.

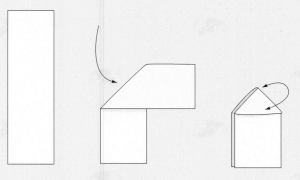

DIAGRAM I

GRANDMOTHER'S HANKIE PURSE

MATERIALS

- 12" square antique blue hankie

- Approximately 10" square antique hankie with monogram

- 12" square of light blue silk for lining

- 4mm blue silk ribbon

- ½ yard of ½"-wide flat lace

- ½ yard of twisted cord for handle

- Light blue pearl rayon thread

- White tassel

- Small glass beads

- Crystal seed beads

- 5" silver purse handle with sew-through holes

PREPARE THE HANKIES

1. Fold the blue hankie diagonally in half; press. Referring to Diagram J, place the monogrammed hankie on top of the folded blue hankie; the edge should be about 1" in from the edge of the blue hankie. Pin the hankies together, and trim the monogrammed hankie ¼" beyond the fold of the blue hankie.

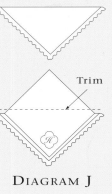

Trim

DIAGRAM J

2. Unpin the hankies. Unfold the blue hankie, place it on a flat surface, and smooth out any wrinkles. Reposition the monogrammed hankie face up on the blue hankie. Place the lining square face down on the two hankies, and pin the three layers together.

3. Lightly mark a diagonal line on the lining square. Starting and stopping 1" from the corners, sew a row of stitches ⅛" on each side of the diagonal, catching the raw edges of the monogrammed hankie in the seam. See Diagram K. Sew across the ends to connect the two rows, creating a ¼"-wide rectangle.

DIAGRAM K

4. Carefully slit the fabric between the stitch lines, and press the lining to the inside. If desired, trim the seam allowance on the monogrammed hankie to ⅛". Sew a row of gathering stitches close to the top edge on both sides of the opening.

5. Sew the lining pieces together along the bottom edge. Using the pearl rayon thread, hand-stitch the blue hankie edges together along the bottom edge.

ASSEMBLE THE PURSE

1. If the purse handle is new and very shiny, you may want to darken it a bit to give it a slightly aged look. Rub a black permanent marker over the handle, then quickly smudge it with tissue. The idea is to have darker and lighter areas; don't completely cover the handle with the marker.

DIAGRAM L

2. Gather the edges of the opening, and hand-stitch the purse to the handle. See Diagram L.

3. Use the silk ribbon to hand-sew a running stitch along the edge of the monogrammed hankie. Hand-stitch the ½"-wide lace around the edge of the hankie.

4. Accent the monogrammed hankie with glass beads and crystal beads as desired. Sew the tassel to the bottom of the blue hankie.

5. Tie the ends of the cord to the handle.

BRIDE'S HANKIE

MATERIALS

- Antique or new white lace-edged hankie
- Scrap of blue moiré fabric for appliqué
- 3mm blue silk ribbon
- Fusible web
- Blue embroidery floss
- ¼" pearl charm or decorative button
- Fabric glue

APPLIQUÉ THE HANKIE

1. Trace the bow pattern on page 92 onto the paper side of the fusible web. Following the manufacturer's instructions, fuse the pattern to the moiré fabric, then cut along the traced lines. Fuse the bow pieces to one corner of the hankie.

2. Using two strands of embroidery floss, blanket-stitch around the appliqués. Glue the pearl charm to the center of the bow.

3. Weave the silk ribbon through the stitching at the edge of the hankie. On the hankie shown, the ribbon is woven through the stitches that secure the lace to the hankie fabric. If you prefer, weave the ribbon through the edge of the lace itself.

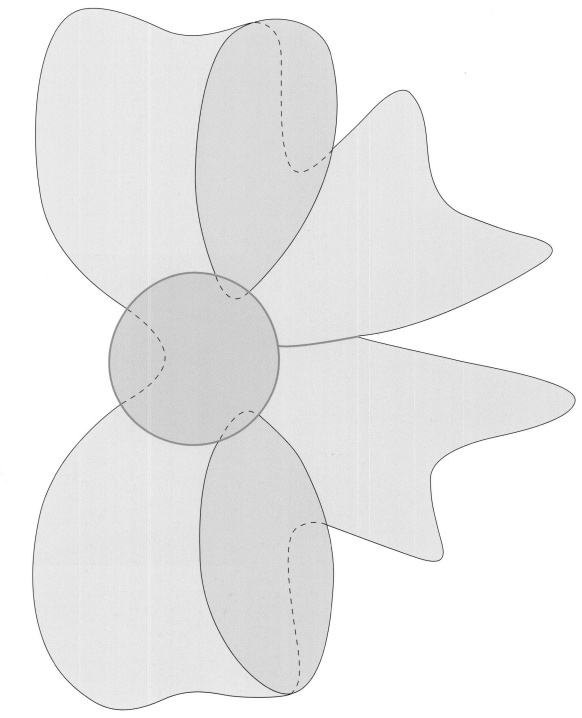

**BOW FOR
FLOWER
GROUPINGS**

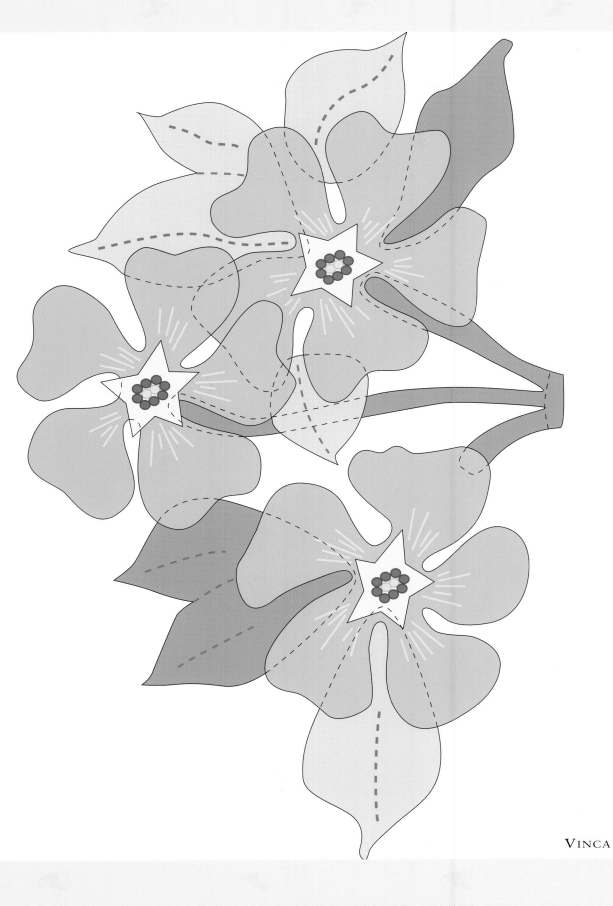

VINCA

ANEMONE

LAURENTIA

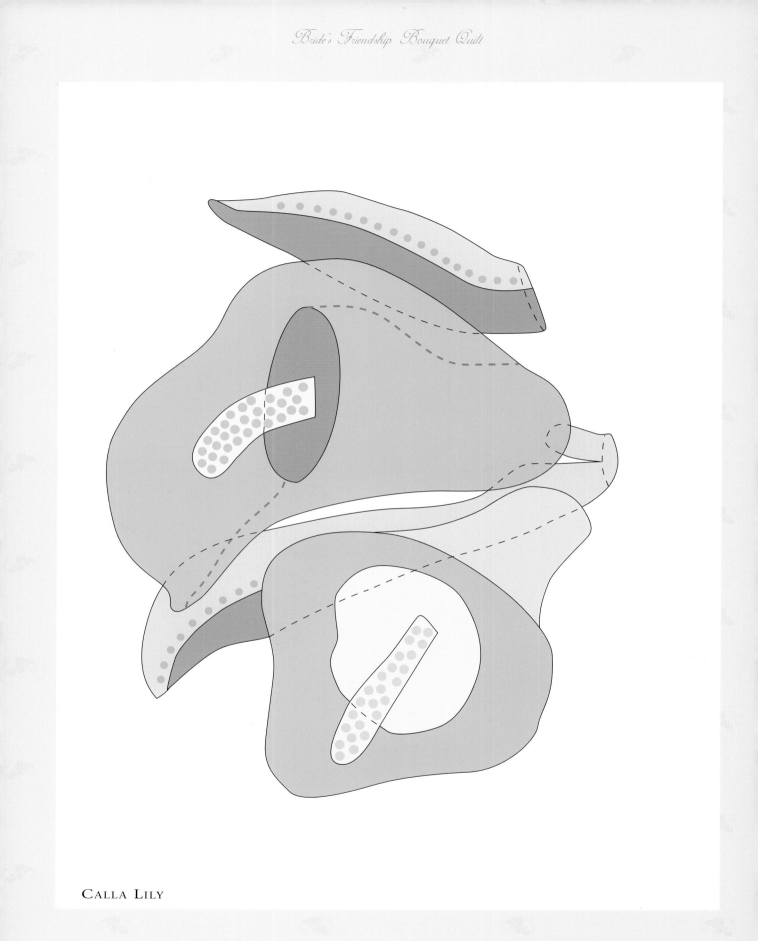

CALLA LILY

COLUMBINE

CONEFLOWER

JAPANESE BELL
FLOWER

PANSY

LILY

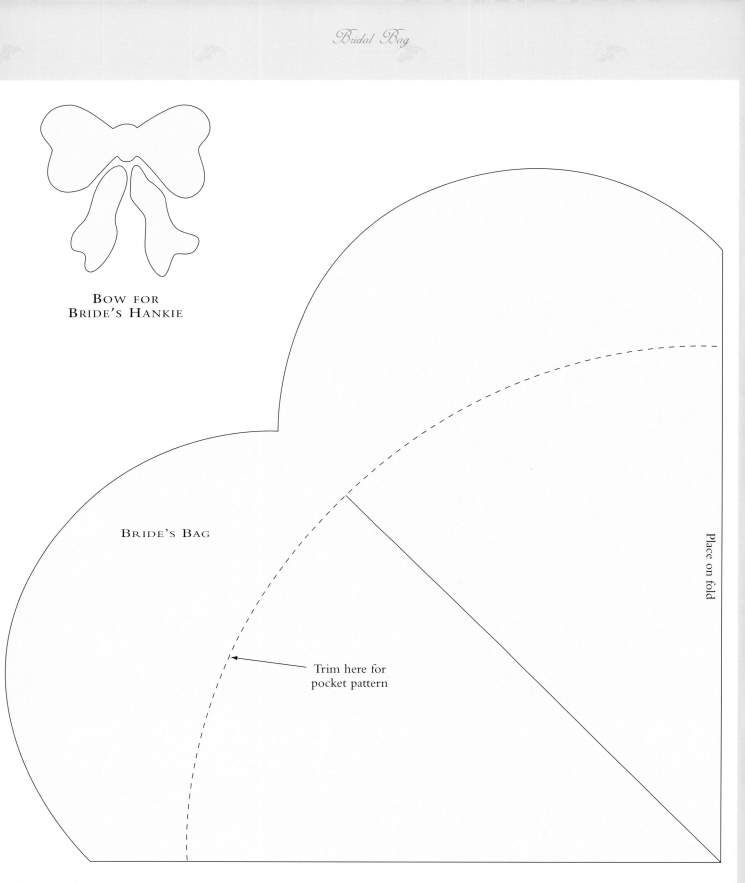

**BOW FOR
BRIDE'S HANKIE**

BRIDE'S BAG

Trim here for
pocket pattern

Place on fold

BRIDAL BAG PATTERN

something · old · new · borrowed & blue

**BRIDAL BAG VERSE
TEMPLATE**
Note: Enlarge template 200% for use.

FAMILY

Families Are Forever

As an old sage once pointed out, "Big oaks from little acorns grow." So it is with "family." Choose from the tablerunner shown here and other inspirations on the following pages to surround yourself with favorite memories of grandparents, aunts, uncles, cousins, moms, dads, and best of all, the children who bring love and laughter to our homes.

The branches of my family tree are filled with memories.
As I add each new name, I'm reminded of all those who've worked
so hard to give our family a future filled with hope, happiness, and love.

FAMILY

or generations, the Tree of Life has been the symbol of hope of new life and rebirth in the spring. The Tree of Life quilt block shown here provides ample opportunity to record new additions to your family tree. Use a permanent marking pen to autograph each completed block or embroider the names in colors to match with two strands of floss.

A trio of blocks can be assembled into the table runner shown on page 96 or made in multiples for a never-to-be-forgotten family tree memory quilt.

ond memories of your grandfather will come flooding back with a Bow Tie patchwork in miniature for your favorite bear to wear. The patchwork bow ties featured on Grandpa Bear's Vest are cut from scraps of ties that were at the height of fashion when Grandpa wore them!

The "little professor" bear shown here is one of my own design, all dressed up in pants and sweater scaled down from the real ones worn by my grandfather and topped off by a vintage bow tie from his closet.

Once you've completed the vest, trim it with awards, pins, charms, and other treasured keepsakes.

Grandmother's Heartstrings Vest is simply a beautiful way to surround yourself with the names or photos of the cutest kids in all the world—your grandchildren!

It's easy to say "I love you" with an appliqué heart for each child cut from white Ultrasuede, embellished with a name, date, or fabric-transfer photo, and trimmed with purchased ribbon roses, French knots, and scraps of lace.

Tie it all together with satin ribbon on a purchased vest or one handmade from your favorite pattern and the grandchildren will be close to your heart forever!

Hearts and flowers are among my favorite motifs for making memories with fabric.

FAMILY

For sisters, a lifetime of sharing makes for a myriad of memories! In a special poem written just for me, my sister Suzanne compares the contrasting lifestyles that have led each of us down a different path. While Suzanne enjoys the great outdoors and life in the country, I'm a "city girl" surrounded with fine china, antiques, and linens all lavished with lace.

However, when we do get together, Suzanne and I love to sit down and share over a hot cup of tea. I use the occasion to make my "city" house a home for the tea cozy complete with a matching napkin. The reverse side of the tea cozy is reserved for an iron-on photo transfer of one of the many antique paintings from my treasury of collectibles.

Margaret & Me

Patterns, scissors and a sewing machine,
Cross stitch bunnies in Easter egg colors,
Calico, chintz and a quilt made of jeans,
These things make up my sister's world.

Bowels and spoons and measuring cups,
Butter and sugar and flour and yeast,
I like to make bread with golden brown crust.
My kitchen is a friendly place to be.

Shops and cafes and bright city lights,
Neat rows of houses with well clipped lawns,
Yards where neighbors talk over the fence,
This is where she has made her home.

Spiderwort, anemones, and roses in ditches,
Pastures with horses and cattle together,
Tractors and disks and pickups with hitches,
I'm sure this is where I'll live forever.

Fine china teacups with saucers that match,
A long afternoon enjoyed over tea,
Green sequin leaves on cottonwood trees,
On these my sister and I agree.

nyone can have custom "art to go" with the ease of permanent markers, basic embroidery stitches, and iron-on fabric transfers. Sort through the stack of kid's drawings that you've saved forever, and take the best of show with you on a tote or T-shirt.

For the quick-to-make tote shown here, a child's whimsical crayon drawing takes center stage on an embroidered quilt block sashed with gingham-checked ribbons.

The fabric transfer method works well for smaller mementos such as fun photos when you sew them to the front of a baseball cap or baby's hat like the one shown here.

ring back memories and display them in a Trip Around the World quilt with a matching photo frame! This clever wall decor quilt features a map of the United States cut from fun new fabric printed with favorite travel destinations. A grid of ¼˝-wide leather lacing on the quilt front provides a quick place to stash postcards and programs.

Transfer special travel keepsakes such as tickets, tokens, and souvenir foreign currency to fabric, and tie the cutouts with ribbons to the buttons scattered across the blocks.

When our three grown children, Robin, Rachel, and Ryan come home to visit, Gary and I enjoy the comments they make when reviewing our family history from the Trip Around the World quilt.

TREE OF LIFE TABLE RUNNER

21" x 63"
12" finished block

MATERIALS

- 2 yards of blue print for sashing, back, and binding

- ¾ yard of green print for blocks and sashing

- ¾ yard of blue-green print for blocks and sashing

- ½ yard of cream tone-on-tone print for blocks

- ¼ yard of brown fabric for blocks

- 25" x 67" batting

- Rotary cutter, ruler, and cutting mat

- Permanent marking pen to autograph blocks

CUTTING

1. From the green print, cut three 3" squares and six 2⅜" squares; cut all the squares in half diagonally. Cut nine 1¾" x 44" strips for sashing. Cut 2¼"-wide bias strips to make triangle squares.

2. From the blue-green print, cut three 2⅜" squares; cut the squares in half diagonally. Cut ten 1¾" x 44" strips for sashing. Cut 2¼"-wide bias strips to make triangle squares.

3. From the cream fabric, cut six A pieces using the pattern on page 123. Cut two 3⅞" squares and three 5⅜" squares; cut all the squares in half diagonally. Cut six 2" squares. Cut 2¼"-wide bias strips to make triangle squares.

4. From the brown fabric, cut three B pieces using the pattern. Cut three 2⅜" squares; cut in half diagonally.

5. From the blue print fabric, cut four 1¾" x 44" strips for sashing. Cut four 2½" x 44" strips for binding; sew together to make one long strip.

PIECE THE BLOCKS

1. To make the triangle squares, sew green and cream bias strips together as shown in Diagram A; press. Make a 2" square template from plastic or cardboard, and use the template to mark and cut triangle squares as shown. If you prefer, use a bias square ruler and a rotary cutter to cut out the squares. You will need a total of 12 green-and-cream squares for each block.

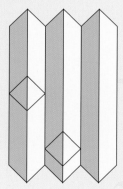

DIAGRAM A

2. In the same manner, sew blue-green and cream strips together, and cut 12 triangle squares for each block from this fabric combination.

3. Referring to the photo and Diagram B, sew triangle squares together in rows; join the rows as shown. To assemble the tree section, sew the green triangles to the A pieces. Sew the brown triangles to the B piece, but stop

sewing ¼" from the outside edge. Sew the A units to the B unit. Add the cream triangle to the corner. Make three blocks.

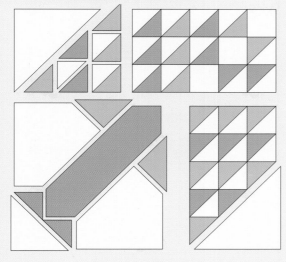

DIAGRAM B

4. Join the units to complete the block. If desired, have family members autograph the blocks using permanent fabric markers.

5. Place a 1¾" blue print sashing strip face down along one edge of the completed block. Stitch with a ¼" seam allowance. Trim the excess strip. Place the strip on the opposite edge of the block, and stitch the sashing in place. Trim the excess.

6. In the same manner, add sashing strips to the two remaining sides of the block. Repeat for all three blocks.

7. Add the 1¾"-wide green and blue-green sashing strips the same way you added the blue print strips. Referring to the photo and Diagram C, sew the strips to the blocks, alternating the colors. Sew a strip to two opposite sides, and press. Sew the same color strip to the two remaining sides; press.

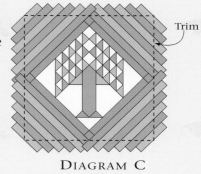

Trim

DIAGRAM C

8. Sew the three blocks together as shown, matching the seams of the sashing strips. Layer the top, batting, and backing; baste. Quilt in the ditch between the blocks, along the sashing strips, and around the block pieces. Bind with the blue print strip.

GRANDPA BEAR'S VEST

MATERIALS

- ⅛ yard each of six different small-scale print fabrics for blocks
- ¼ yard each of three different solid fabrics for blocks
- ¼ yard of print fabric for lining
- Two ⅜" buttons
- Assorted small charms such as key, pins, tie tack
- Freezer paper

PIECE THE BLOCKS

1. Cut two print and two solid 1¾" squares for each Bow Tie block. Cut one 1¼" matching print square for the center "knot." You will need a total of 32 blocks.

2. Piece the squares into four-patch blocks. To add the center squares, cut one ¾" square of freezer paper for each block. Center the freezer paper, waxy side out, on the wrong side of the 1¼" squares. Fold the seam allowance over the freezer paper and press. Position the square face down on the four-patch block and appliqué in place. Cut a tiny slit in the back of the block, taking care not to cut through the top layer. Remove the freezer paper using tweezers.

3. Lay out the Bow Tie blocks in a rectangle with eight blocks across and four blocks down. See Diagram D. Position the blocks so that half are facing one direction and half are facing the opposite direction. This way, the bow ties will be facing each other at the center front of the vest.

ASSEMBLE THE VEST

1. Fold the pieced rectangle in half, wrong sides together. Using the   pattern on page 121, trace and cut out the vest from the patchwork. Before you cut, check to see that the center back of the vest is right at the center seamline of the pieced rectangle.

2. Using the pattern, cut a vest lining from print fabric.

3. Pin the vest and the lining right sides together. Using a ¼" seam allowance, stitch the neck edge, armhole curves, front curve, and bottom edge, leaving an opening for turning. Do not stitch the shoulder seams. Clip the seams, and turn right side out through the opening. Stitch the shoulder seams and press the seam allowances open.

4. Topstitch all the way around the vest, stitching close to the outer edge. Trim excess seam allowance at the shoulders. Add buttons and buttonholes. Add charms and pins.

DIAGRAM D

GRANDMOTHER'S HEARTSTRINGS VEST

MATERIALS

- Favorite vest pattern or purchased vest*

- Blue fabric and lining fabric according to pattern

- ⅛ yard of white Ultrasuede for hearts

- Low-loft batting

- 5" x 7" white lace panel with heart cutout

- 1½ yards each of two different flat lace trims

- 18 purchased flower appliqués

- 3 yards of ¼"-wide blue satin ribbon

- 7mm pink silk ribbon

- Three ½" pink shank heart buttons

- ½" white pearl sew-through heart beads

- ⅝" clear sew-through heart beads

- ⅝" rhinestone heart charms

- Rayon floss in assorted colors

The project was made using McCall's Pattern #8699.

ASSEMBLE THE VEST

1. Cut out the vest and vest lining pieces and assemble according to the pattern instructions. If desired, insert a layer of low-loft batting between the vest fabric and the lining.

2. Using the pattern on page 123, lightly trace nine hearts onto the white Ultrasuede, leaving a ½" space between them. Embroider the heart outlines as desired, then cut out the hearts with pinking shears, cutting about ⅛" beyond the stitch line. Embroider grandchildren's names and birthdates. Embroider extra hearts as desired.

3. Sew the lace trims to the vest lapels, and add the flower appliqués.

4. Cut the ¼"-wide blue ribbon in half. Referring to the photo, arrange one ribbon on each side of the vest front, looping it very casually down the front. Keep it very loose and flowing. Pin the ribbon in a few places to hold it while you add the other elements.

5. Cut nine hearts from batting using the pattern, then trim them so they are about ⅛" smaller than the pattern. Place one embroidered heart on each batting heart; arrange eight hearts on top of the ribbons on the vest front; pin. Topstitch in place, stitching just inside the pinked edge.

6. Sew the beads and buttons to the vest fronts as desired. Stitch some on top of the ribbons, and others alongside.

7. Weave the pink ribbon around the outside edge of the lace panel, and tie it in a bow. Center the panel on the vest back. Topstitch around the outside edge, and around the opening. Center the remaining heart in the opening, topstitch in place. Add four appliqués as shown.

HOME SWEET HOME TEA COZY AND NAPKIN

MATERIALS

- ½ yard of yellow moiré taffeta for background, back, and piping

- ½ yard of yellow fabric for lining

- ⅛ yard each of assorted print fabrics for roof

- 12" square of 32-count cross-stitch fabric for napkin

- Assorted scraps for windows, door, and flower appliqués

- Lightweight batting

- Light and dark pink, light and dark purple, green, and tan embroidery floss

- 1¾ yards of ⅛" cord for piping

- 2" lace heart

- Purchased heart appliqué

- Tiny gold bell

- Tiny heart button

- Freezer paper

PREPARE THE FRONT

1. Trace the house shape and detail onto yellow moiré taffeta using the pattern on page 122. Cut out at least 1" beyond the outline on all sides. Trace and cut a second piece of moiré for the back.

2. Trace and cut 20 clamshells from print fabrics using the pattern on page 123. Trace and cut 20 clamshells from freezer paper using the inner dashed line on the pattern. Place a freezer paper clamshell, waxy side out, on the wrong side of each fabric clamshell. Fold the fabric seam allowance over the edge of the paper template, and press.

3. Referring to the pattern, position and pin a row of five clamshells onto the yellow moiré front. Hand appliqué the clamshells in place, stitching along the lower, curved edge. Leave the top end unstitched; it will be covered by the next row of clamshells. Remove the templates by pulling them through the openings at the top of the clamshells. Position and appliqué the next row of clamshells; remove the paper templates. Add a total of four rows of clamshells to complete the roof.

4. Referring to the photo and the pattern, hand appliqué the door, windows, shutters, and flowers. Embroider the flower centers with straight stitch and French knots. Embroider the leaves and grass in straight stitch. Add the flowerbuds and vines in outline stitch, satin stitch, and French knots. Use the tan floss and an outline stitch to embroider the address.

ASSEMBLE THE TEA COZY

1. Line the front with batting and quilt as desired. Baste along the outline of the cozy, then cut out ¼" beyond the outline. Quilt the back as desired, and cut to the same size as the front. Cut two lining pieces to the same size as the outside front and back.

2. Cut 1½"-wide bias strips from the yellow moiré and sew together into one strip about 63" long. Cover the cord with the bias strip, using a zipper foot and a ½" seam allowance. Trim the seam allowance to ¼".

3. Stitch the piping along the sides and top of the tea cozy front, clipping the seam allowance as necessary. Stitch a small piping loop at the top of the cozy. To make the loop, cut a ½" x 2" bias strip. Turn under one long edge about ¼", and press. Wrap the strip around a piece of cord, and hand stitch the folded edge to secure.

4. Place the front and back right sides together and stitch along the sides and top. Trim and clip the seam allowance. Repeat for the front and back lining pieces. Turn right side out.

5. Stitch piping around the bottom edge. Place the cozy and the lining right sides together, matching the side seams. Stitch around the bottom edge, leaving an opening for turning. Trim and clip the seam. Turn right side out

through the opening, and stitch the opening closed. Press the lining along the bottom edge and hand-tack in several places along the side seam.

6. Add the heart button for a door knob. Add the purchased lace heart and heart appliqué to the door.

ASSEMBLE THE NAPKIN

1. Using the flower patterns from the tea cozy, appliqué the flowers at one corner about 2" up from the point.

2. Place a length of 6-ply pink floss around the outside of the napkin, about ¾" from the outer edge, and machine zigzag over it. Fringe the outer edge about ½".

Margaret & Me

Patterns, scissors and a sewing machine,
Cross stitch bunnies in Easter egg colors,
Calico, chintz and a quilt made of jeans,
These things make up my sister's world.

Bowls and spoons and measuring cups,
Butter and sugar and flour and yeast,
I like to make bread with golden brown crust.
My kitchen is a friendly place to be.

Shops and cafes and bright city lights,
Neat rows of houses with well clipped lawns,
Yards where neighbors talk over the fence,
This is where she has made her home.

Spiderwort, anenomes, and roses in ditches,
Pastures with horses and cattle together,
Tractors and disks and pickups with hitches,
I'm sure this is where I'll live forever.

Fine china teacups with saucers that match,
A long afternoon enjoyed over tea,
Green sequin leaves on cottonwood trees,
On these my sister and I agree.

QUILTED TOTE BAG
10½" x 10½" x 3"

MATERIALS

- ⅝ yard of red plaid fabric for sides, back, and handles
- ½ yard of yellow gingham fabric for lining
- 11" square of light yellow fabric
- ⅝ yard of 1"-wide yellow check ribbon
- ⅜ yard each of 1"-wide green check and blue check ribbons
- ¾ yard of ½"-wide floral woven ribbon
- Wide yellow rickrack
- Lightweight batting
- Child's drawing
- Four ⅝" heart buttons
- Four ⅜" flower buttons
- Embroidery floss in assorted colors
- Permanent fabric pen

CUTTING

1. From the red plaid fabric, cut one 11" square and one 3½" x 32" strip. Cut two 2½" x 13½" strips for handles.

2. From the yellow gingham fabric, cut two 11" squares and one 3½" x 32" strip.

3. From the batting, cut two 11" squares and one 3½" x 32" strip. Cut two ½" x 13" strips for the handles.

4. From the yellow check ribbon, cut two 11" lengths. From the blue and green check ribbons, cut one 11" length each.

PREPARE THE BAG FRONT

1. Using a permanent fabric marker, trace a child's drawing onto the light yellow square. Outline some of the drawing's elements with embroidery floss, using a running stitch and assorted colors as desired. Use the photo for inspiration; since your drawing will be different, your embroidery will be, too. If you wish, add small ribbons and buttons to the drawing as appropriate.

2. Place the yellow square on top of one 11" square of batting; baste. Position the blue check and green check ribbons at the top and bottom of the block, making sure the outer edge is a generous ¼" from the edge of the block. See Diagram E. The raw ends of the

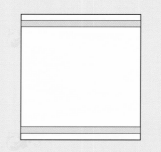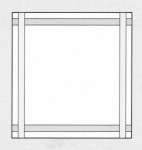

DIAGRAM E

ribbons should be even with the sides of the block. Pin, then topstitch the ribbons in place, stitching very close to both long edges.

3. In the same manner, position the yellow check ribbons on the sides of the block, overlapping the blue and green ribbons. Make sure the outer edges are a generous ¼" from the sides of the block, and that the ends are even with the top and bottom. Top-stitch the ribbons in place.

ASSEMBLE THE TOTE BAG

1. Place the 11" red plaid square (the bag back) on top of the remaining 11" square of batting. Pin, then quilt as desired.

2. Place the 3½"-wide red plaid strip on top of the matching batting strip; machine-baste the layers together.

3. Beginning at one top corner and using a ¼" seam allowance, sew the red plaid side strip to the sides and bottom of the quilted back. Clip the corners as necessary, and trim the batting from the seam allowance. In the same manner, sew the strip to the completed front, taking care not to catch the edge of the ribbons in the seam allowance.

4. Sew the rickrack around the top edge of the bag.

5. To make the handles, turn under ¼" along both long edges of the handle strips; press. Fold the strips in half lengthwise, wrong sides together, and press. Unfold and slip a strip of batting into each handle. Fold the fabric over the batting, and topstitch very close to the edge of the strip. Center the floral ribbon on the handle, and topstitch along both edges of the ribbon.

6. Position the handles on the bag front and back with the outside edges of the handles about 2" in from the side edges of the front and back panels. Baste the handles in place, having the ends even with the top raw edge of the bag.

7. Sew the lining pieces together in the same manner as for the bag, but leave an opening along one side for turning.

8. Place the bag and the lining right sides together, matching the seams. Stitch around the top edge, then turn right side out through the opening in the lining. Stitch the opening closed.

9. Press the lining to the inside. Topstitch through all layers along the top edge to hold the lining in place.

10. Add buttons and trims to the bag front as desired.

Personalize a cap for baby with eye-catching photos from your family album.

TRIP AROUND THE WORLD QUILT

35½" square including prairie points

MATERIALS

- 1½ yards of print fabric for map, backing, and prairie points*
- ¾ yard of sage fabric for center panel
- ¼ yard each of eight different solid fabrics for patchwork
- Lightweight batting
- 10 yards of ¼"-wide leather lacing
- Pearl cotton
- 120 sew-through buttons
- Tracing paper
- Rayon thread
- Fusible web

The vacation print fabric and coordinating solids are from Robert Kaufman Co., Inc. See Sources for details.

CUTTING

1. From the print fabric, cut one 32½" square for the quilt back, and cut sixty-four 4" squares for prairie points.

2. From the solid fabrics, cut 2½" squares according to the following chart:

Color 1	Gold	32 squares
Color 2	Meadow	28
Color 3	Cerise	24
Color 4	Sienna	20
Color 5	Willow	16
Color 6	Lotus	12
Color 7	Crimson	8
Color 8	Jade	32

3. From the sage fabric, cut one 20½" square for center panel background.

PIECE THE QUILT TOP

1. Trace the outline of the United States from a map or a book. Enlarge the shape to about 14" x 19", so that it fits in the center panel when it's turned on point. Trace the shape in reverse onto the paper side of the fusible web. Cut just outside the traced lines. Following the manufacturer's instructions, fuse to the wrong side of the print fabric. Cut out on the traced lines, and fuse the map to the sage background square. Machine appliqué the map using matching thread.

2. Referring to Diagram F, arrange the squares into four identical corner units. Sew the squares together in rows, then join the rows to complete each corner.

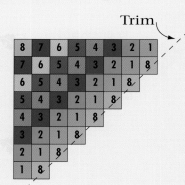

DIAGRAM F

3. Trim the row of Color 8 blocks on each corner, leaving a ¼" seam allowance. Sew the corners to the center panel as shown in Diagram G. Complete the seams at the outer edge.

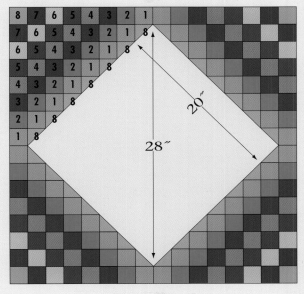

DIAGRAM G

ASSEMBLE THE QUILT

1. To make prairie points, fold the 4" squares in half diagonally, wrong sides together; press. Fold in half again, aligning the raw edges; press. Divide the prairie points into four sets of 16 triangles each. Referring to Diagram H, tuck the folded edge of each triangle between the ends of the adjacent triangle, overlapping about halfway; pin together. Stitch the prairie points together in four strips.

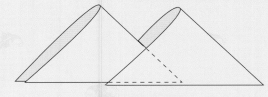

DIAGRAM H

2. Baste the batting to the wrong side of the quilt top. With raw edges aligned, stitch the prairie points to the right side of the quilt top, stitching the batting in place at the same time.

3. Place the quilt back face down on the quilt top, with the prairie points between the layers; pin. Stitch with a ¼" seam allowance, leaving an opening for turning. Trim the corners. Turn the quilt right side out and stitch the opening closed.

4. Machine quilt around the map and in the ditch at the edge of the center panel. Sew a button at the corner of each square.

5. Cut 12 leather strips, each a generous 20" long. Arrange six strips, evenly spaced, across the center panel; machine tailor-tack the ends in place. Weave the remaining six strips in the opposite direction, and tailor-tack the ends. Tack several of the intersections to secure the strips.

PRAIRIE POINTS PHOTO FRAME

MATERIALS

- 10" x 12" piece of print fabric for front

- 10" x 12" piece of sage fabric for back

- 8" x 10" piece of sage fabric for back lining

- Assorted scraps of solid fabrics for prairie points

- 1¼ yards of ½"-wide flat green braid

- Extra-loft fleece

- Two 8" x 10" self-adhesive mounting boards*

- 8" x 10" gold mat

- One ½" x 4½" and two ½" x 8" strips of foamcore

- Fabric glue

- Purchased easel

The project shown was made with Crescent Perfect Mount self-adhesive mounting board. See Sources for details.

ASSEMBLE THE FRAME

1. Mark and cut a 4½" x 5½" opening in the center of one of the mounting boards. Mark a 3¾"x 4¾" opening in the center of the gold mat; cut.

2. Glue two layers of fleece onto the front of the cut mounting board. Cut out the center of the fleece even with the opening.

3. Center the fleece-covered mat face down on the wrong side of the print fabric. Wrap the excess fabric to the back side, mitering the corners; glue. Cut a 2½" x 3½" rectangle from

the center of the fabric. Slit the remaining fabric into the corners of the opening. See Diagram I. Pull the excess fabric through the opening to the back side and glue securely. Center and glue the padded frame to the gold mat.

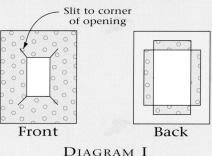

Slit to corner of opening

Front   Back

DIAGRAM I

4. Cut an assortment of 2½" squares from the solid fabrics; you will need 28 squares. Make prairie points and arrange them in rows as described in Step 1 under Assemble the Quilt, on page 119. Make two rows of eight and two rows of six. Stitch the prairie points into chains, then glue them around the outside edge of the padded mat.

5. Glue the foamcore strips to the back of the mat along the sides and bottom. Cover the back mounting board with sage fabric. Glue the covered back to the foamcore strips.

6. Glue the flat braid around the edge of the padded mat. Add souvenir coins and tokens as desired. Insert the photo from the top. Place the frame on the purchased easel.

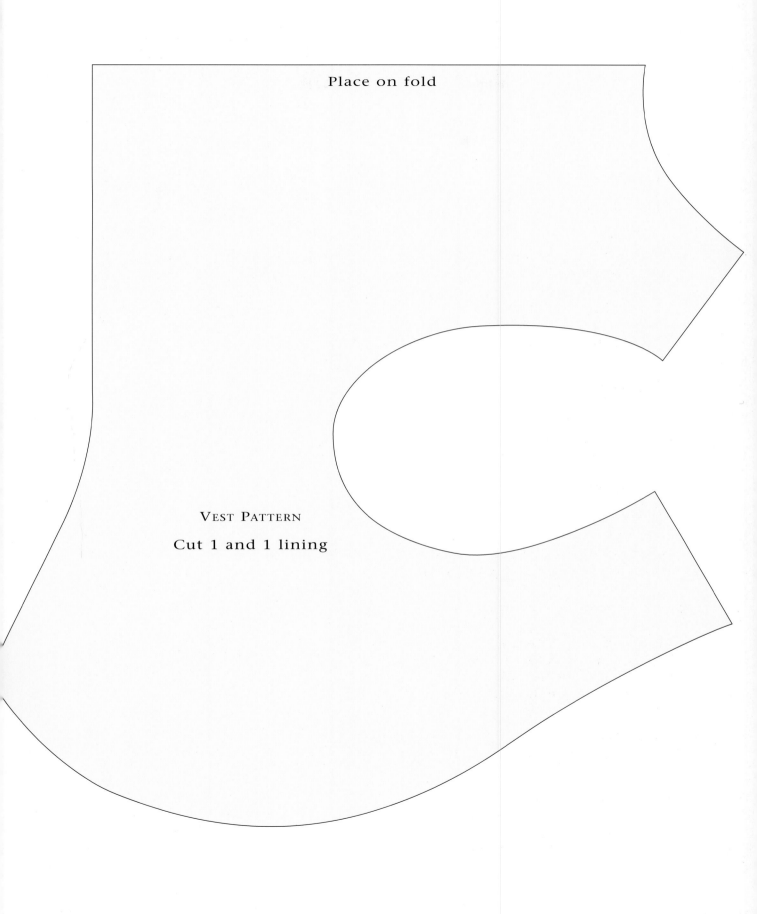

Place on fold

Vest Pattern

Cut 1 and 1 lining

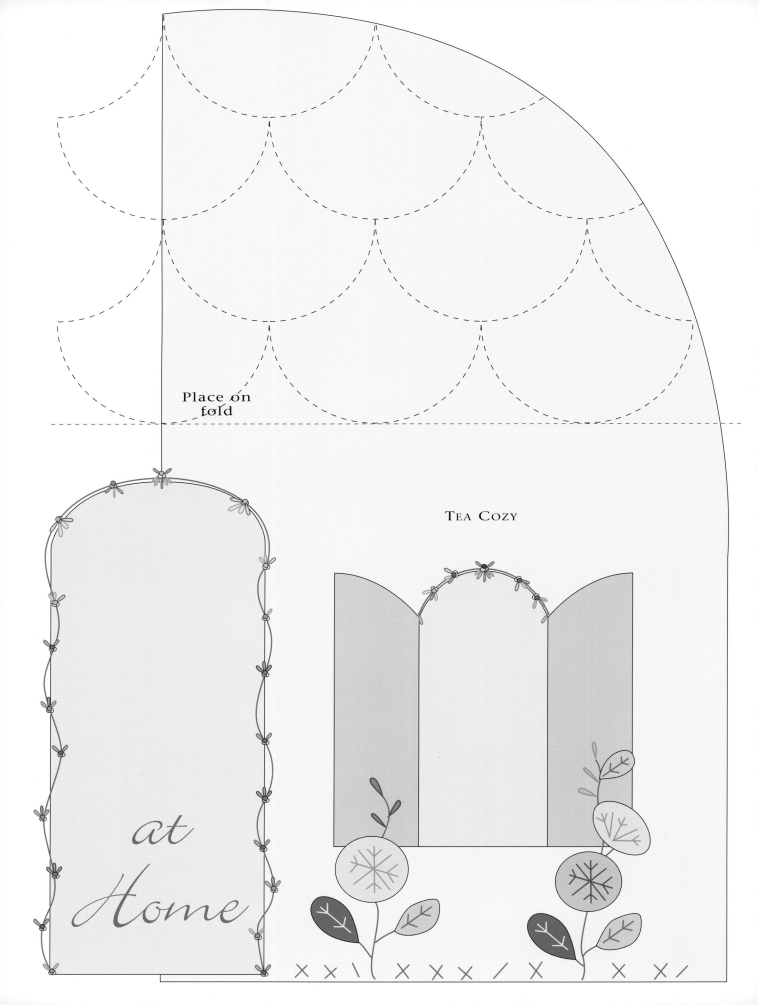

Place on
fold

Tea Cozy

at

Home

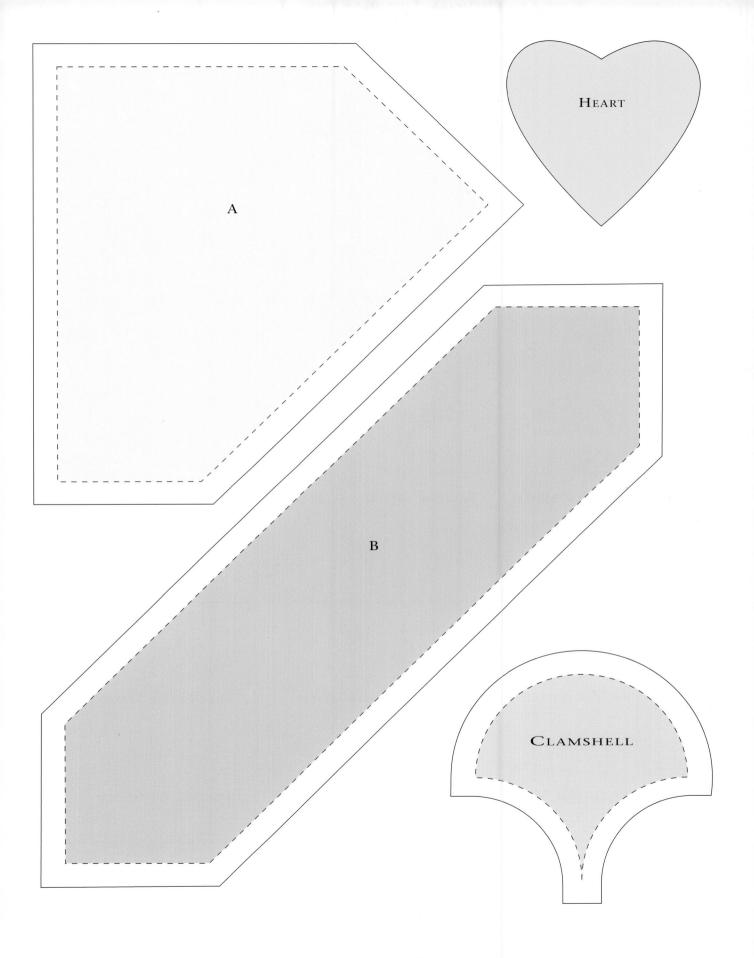

A

B

HEART

CLAMSHELL

STITCH GUIDE

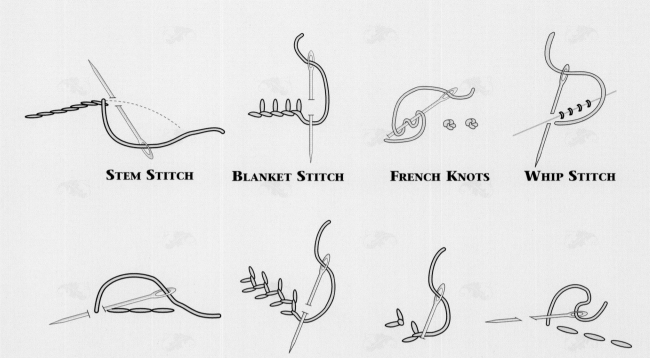

STEM STITCH   **BLANKET STITCH**   **FRENCH KNOTS**   **WHIP STITCH**

BACK STITCH   **FEATHER STITCH**   **FLY STITCH**   **RUNNING STITCH**

MACHINE-APPLIQUÉ STITCHES

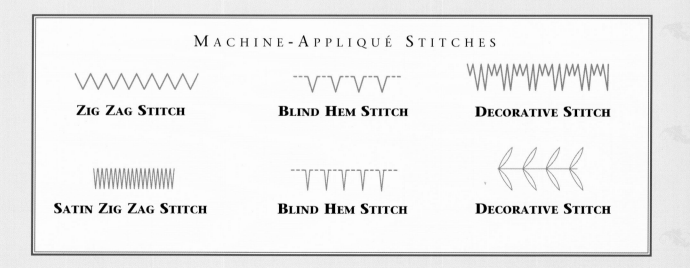

ZIG ZAG STITCH   **BLIND HEM STITCH**   **DECORATIVE STITCH**

SATIN ZIG ZAG STITCH   **BLIND HEM STITCH**   **DECORATIVE STITCH**

GLOSSARY

APPLIQUÉ As a noun it refers to a piece of fabric that is placed on a background either by sewing or, as instructed many times in this book, by fusing. As a verb, it refers to the process of securing a piece of fabric on the background.

BACKING The bottom layer (back) of a quilt.

BASTING Temporary stitches or pins, holding the quilt layers together.

BATTING The filling between two layers of fabric. It contributes warmth to a quilt, and structure to wallhangings and clothing. Batting comes in a variety of lofts (thicknesses) and fibers (wool, cotton, or polyester, or a combination).

BIAS The diagonal grain of the fabric; usually at a 45° angle to the selvage.

BINDING A fabric strip that encloses the layers at the edge of a quilt.

BORDER One or more fabric strips that frame the center part of a quilt top.

CRAZY QUILT Irregular-shaped pieces sewn onto a foundation fabric, usually embellished with embroidery stitches.

EMBROIDERY Decorative hand- or machine-stitching using thread or yarn.

FUSIBLE WEB A product consisting of a layer of heat sensitive fibers and a paper layer to facilitate construction.

PHOTO TRANSFER The process of transferring a photo or illustration to fabric. The image can either be photocopied or printed out of a computer, depending on the transfer paper used and the manufacturer's instructions.

QUILT As a noun it refers to a top layered with batting and backing and held together with stitches. As a verb it refers to the process of securing the layers with small hand- or machine-stitches and is usually done in a pattern.

REVERSE To turn a pattern over to cut the design in the opposite direction.

SEAM ALLOWANCE The space between the stitching line and the edge of the fabric.

TEMPLATE A pattern made from plastic or cardboard, used as a guide for marking and transferring the pattern shape onto fabric by tracing around it.

BABY PRINT FABRIC: The fabric used to make the Monday's Child quilt on page 28 is from David Textiles. For more information or to locate the nearest retailer, contact: David Textiles, Inc., 5959 Telegraph Road, City of Commerce, CA 90040.

BUTTON FORMS, SEWING BOX: Look for Prym-Dritz products at sewing and craft stores. To locate the nearest retailer, contact: Prym-Dritz Corporation, P.O. Box 5028, Spartanburg, SC 29304, (800) 255-7796. The button forms used on page 74 are the Standard Half-Ball Button. The sewing basket on page 67 is the Naturals 11" x 6⅝" x 6½" rectangle basket (item Z10000).

CROSS-STITCH FABRIC: The fabric used in the box lid on page 32 is 32-count Belfast linen from Zweigart. For more information or to locate the nearest retailer, contact: Zweigart, 2 Riverview Drive, Somerset, NJ 08873, (908) 271-1949.

CRYSTAL BEADS, GLASS BEADS, SEED BEADS: Look for these Mill Hill products, including the Glass & Crystal Treasures collection, in craft and needlework shops. To locate the nearest retailer, contact: Gay Bowles Sales-Mill Hill, P.O. Box 1060, Janesville, WI 53547, (608) 754-9466.

DOUBLE-MATTED FRAME: The frame used on page 20 is the 11" x 14" La Triomph Wall Frame (item 110176) from Exposures. For more information or a mail-order catalog, call (800) 222-4947.

HAND-DYED SILK RIBBONS: The ribbons used to make the flowers on page 67 are hand-dyed, bias-cut silk ribbons from Hanah Silk. For more information, call (888) 233-5187.

IRON-ON FABRIC SHEETS: Look for ComputerCrafts Iron-On Fabric Sheets from Janlynn Cre8. To locate the nearest retailer write The Janlynn Corporation, 34 Front Street, PO Box 51848, Indian Orchard, MA 01152. For online help, tips, and techniques, visit the Janlynn website at www.makeitcool.com.

MINI BRASS FRAMES, RHINESTONE HEART CHARMS, PURSE HANDLE: For information on these items and more, contact: Small Enchantments, P.O. Box 65483, West Des Moines, IA 50265.

MOIRÉ TAFFETA FABRIC: Ribbons, needles, moiré and a whole range of embroidery supplies are available from Bucilla. To locate the nearest retailer, contact: Bucilla Corporation, 1 Oak Ridge Road, Hazelton, PA 18201, (717) 384-2525.

MOUNTING BOARD: Crescent Perfect Mount Self-Adhesive Mounting Board (used in vacation frame) Crescent Cardboard Co. 100 W. Willow Rd., Wheeling, IL 60090, (847) 537-3400.

PEARL COTTON AND EMBROIDERY FLOSS: Look for DMC threads at your favorite craft or needlework shop. To locate the nearest DMC retailer, contact: DMC Corporation, Port Kearney Building 10, South Kearny, NJ 07032.

PHOTO TRANSFER PAPER: The photo transfer paper used on pages 10 and 35 is the Creative Copy™ Photo Transfer Paper by Quiltmakers. For more information, contact: Quiltmakers, 9658 Plano Road, Dallas, TX 75238, (888) 494-0291.

PICTURE FRAME BOX: The box used on page 32 is the 6¼" x 8¼" Picture Frame Box (item 99701) from Sudberry House. Look for this and other Sudberry House products at your favorite needlework or craft shop. To locate the nearest retailer, contact: Sudberry House, P.O. Box 895, Old Lyme, CT 06371.

PILLOW FORMS, BATTING, AND STUFFING: Look for these and other Morning Glory products at your favorite sewing or craft store. To locate the nearest retailer, contact: Morning Glory Products, 302 Highland Drive, Taylor, TX 76574, (800) 234-9105.

RAYON THREAD FOR MACHINE APPLIQUÉ: Coats & Clark, 30 Patewood Drive, #351, Greenville, SC 29615.

SILK RIBBONS: YLI Corporation, 161 W. Main Street Rock Hill, NC 29730, (803) 985-3100.

VACATION PRINT FABRIC: The print fabric and all the solid fabrics used in the Trip Around the World Quilt on page 109 and the Prairie Points Photo Frame on page 108 are from Robert Kaufman Company. For more information or to locate the nearest retailer, contact: Robert Kaufman Co., Inc., 129 West 132nd Street, Los Angeles, CA 90061, (310) 538-3482.

VIKING #1 PLUS SEWING MACHINE: 11760 Berea Road, Cleveland, OH, 44111, (216) 252-3300.

PROJECT INDEX

SELECTED PUBLICATIONS FROM MARTINGALE & CO.

QUILT DESIGN
All New! Copy Art for Quilters illustrated by Barb Tourtillotte
Color: The Quilter's Guide by Christine Barnes
Design Essentials: The Quilter's Guide by Lorraine Torrence
Design Your Own Quilts by Judy Hopkins
Fine Art Quilts: Work by Artists of the Contemporary Quilt Art Association
Freedom in Design by Mia Rozmyn
The Log Cabin Design Workbook by Christal Carter
The Nature of Design by Joan Colvin
QuiltSkills: Workshops from the Quilters' Guild Australia
Surprising Designs from Traditional Quilt Blocks by Carole M. Fure
Whimsies & Whynots by Mary Lou Weidman

FINISHING TECHNIQUES
Borders by Design by Paulette Peters
The Border Workbook by Janet Kime
A Fine Finish by Cody Mazuran
Happy Endings by Mimi Dietrich
Interlacing Borders by Donna Hussain
Loving Stitches by Jeana Kimball
Press for Success by Myrna Giesbrecht
Quilting Design Sourcebook by Dorothy Osler
Quilting Makes the Quilt by Lee Cleland
Sensational Settings by Joan Hanson
Traditional Quilts with Painless Borders by Sally Schneider and Barbara J. Eikmeier
The Ultimate Book of Quilt Labels by Margo J. Clabo

FOUNDATION/PAPER PIECING
Classic Quilts with Precise Foundation Piecing by Tricia Lund and Judy Pollard
Crazy but Pieceable by Hollie A. Milne
Easy Machine Paper Piecing by Carol Doak
Easy Mix & Match Machine Paper Piecing by Carol Doak
Easy Paper-Pieced Keepsake Quilts by Carol Doak
Easy Paper-Pieced Miniatures by Carol Doak
Easy Reversible Vests by Carol Doak
Go Wild with Quilts by Margaret Rolfe
Go Wild with Quilts—Again! by Margaret Rolfe
A Quilter's Ark by Margaret Rolfe
Show Me How to Paper Piece by Carol Doak

HOME DECORATING
Decorate with Quilts & Collections by Nancy J. Martin
The Home Decorator's Stamping Book by Linda Barker
Living with Little Quilts by Alice Berg, Mary Ellen Von Holt, and Sylvia Johnson
Make Room for Quilts by Nancy J. Martin
Soft Furnishings for Your Home by Sharyn Skrabanich
Welcome Home: Debbie Mumm

MACHINE QUILTING/SEWING
Machine Needlelace and Other Embellishment Techniques by Judy Simmons
Machine Quilting Made Easy by Maurine Noble
Machine Quilting with Decorative Threads by Maurine Noble and Elizabeth Hendricks
Thread Magic by Ellen Anne Eddy
Threadplay with Libby Lehman

ROTARY CUTTING/SPEED PIECING
A New Slant on Bargello Quilts by Marge Edie
Around the Block with Judy Hopkins
All-Star Sampler by Roxanne Carter
Bargello Quilts by Marge Edie
Basic Quiltmaking Techniques for Strip Piecing by Paulette Peters
Blockbender Quilts by Margaret J. Miller
Block by Block by Beth Donaldson
Class-Act Quilts
Down the Rotary Road with Judy Hopkins
Easy Seasonal Wall Quilts by Deborah J. Moffett-Hall
Easy Star Sampler by Roxanne Carter
The Joy of Quilting by Joan Hanson and Mary Hickey
Lively Little Logs by Donna Fite McConnell
Magic Base Blocks for Unlimited Quilt Designs by Patty Barney and Cooky Schock
Mirror Manipulations by Gail Valentine
More Quilts for Baby by Ursula Reikes
More Strip-Pieced Watercolor Magic by Deanna Spingola
Patchwork Pantry by Suzette Halferty and Carol C. Porter
A Perfect Match by Donna Lynn Thomas
Quilting Up a Storm by Lydia Quigley
Quilts for Baby by Ursula Reikes
Rotary Riot by Judy Hopkins and Nancy J. Martin
Rotary Roundup by Judy Hopkins and Nancy J. Martin
Shortcuts by Donna Lynn Thomas
Simply Scrappy Quilts by Nancy J. Martin
Square Dance by Martha Thompson
Start with Squares by Martha Thompson
Strip-Pieced Watercolor Magic by Deanna Spingola
Stripples by Donna Lynn Thomas
Stripples Strikes Again! by Donna Lynn Thomas
Strips that Sizzle by Margaret J. Miller
Two-Color Quilts by Nancy J. Martin

STITCHERY/NEEDLE ARTS
Christmas Ribbonry by Camela Nitschke
Hand-Stitched Samplers from I Done My Best by Saundra White
Miniature Baltimore Album Quilts by Jenifer Buechel
A Passion for Ribbonry by Camela Nitschke
A Silk-Ribbon Album by Jenifer Buechel
Victorian Elegance by Lezette Thomason

SURFACE DESIGN/FABRIC MANIPULATION
15 Beads: A Guide to Creating One-of-a-Kind Beads by Jane Dunnewold
The Art of Handmade Paper and Collage by Cheryl Stevenson
Complex Cloth by Jane Dunnewold
Dyes & Paints: A Hands-On Guide to Coloring Fabric by Elin Noble
Hand-Dyed Fabric Made Easy by Adriene Buffington

Many of these books are available through your local fabric, quilt, or craft shop. For more information, call, write, fax, or e-mail for our free full-color catalog.

Martingale & Company
Toll-free: 1-800-426-3126
International: 1-425-483-3313
24-Hour Fax: 1-425-486-7596
PO Box 118
Bothell, WA 98041-0118 USA
Web site: www.patchwork.com
E-mail: info@patchwork.com